A BEAUTIFUL BAG OF FISH

A BEAUTIFUL BAG OF FISH

To preserve his own safety, the author has adopted a pseudonym

Although inspired by actual events, the places and characters in this book have been changed to protect the privacy of others. I have changed the locations and lots of the police methodology and I have also been careful not to divulge any sensitive information. The scenarios in this book are for purposes of entertainment only and may have elements of fiction included in them to increase entertainment value.

I dedicate this book to my wife and children, who for the last several years have listened to my garbage and have helped to put me back on track.
I also dedicate it to all the honest police officers currently working in the United Kingdom, my therapist who encouraged me to write this book and Bhagavan Sri Ramana Maharshi.

Table of contents

I feel it closing in,

I feel it closing in,

Day in, day out,

Day in, day out...

Joy Division - Digital

Introduction

I wouldn't have even considered writing a book if I wasn't finding my soul again—a soul which seemingly deserted my body while growing up in the north of England, which the politicians now sarcastically call The Northern Powerhouse. My soul had probably been buried under all the crap before I joined the police, but it was ripped to shreds and completely locked away after gangsters put a contract out on my life.

When my wife found out that I was writing this book, she said, 'You will need to structure it right because if anybody reads it, they will end up as screwed up as you.' I couldn't stop smiling to myself after hearing this comment, because my gorgeous wife has lived with my issues for years and apart from being my best friend, soulmate and the mother to my two wonderful daughters—she has been my rock, and when required, her mind has adapted to be as crazy as mine.

With little education, I ended up working in a factory for ten years, then as a police officer for twenty-five years. I received several Judges' and Chief Constables' commendations during my time in the police but soon realised that when I asked for help, I was treated only as a number and there was no genuine care given towards myself, or my family.

Toward the end of my police career, a psychiatrist diagnosed me with Complex PTSD, which had been left untreated after being spotted by a welfare officer 11 years before. During these 11 years I worked on drug units and fought with machete-wielding criminals. I also worked undercover, buying heroin, crack cocaine and associated with drug addicts, while trying to stay one step ahead of the dealers.... and the police! All these experiences are included in this book.

Without any treatment or guidance, it was a stolen bag of dead fish which eventually made me wake up to discover who 'I' really was. However, could this be enough? Is being consciousness enough? Or is the conditioned mind too addictive? I suppose it's up to me to find out.

I hope you enjoy your read.

Chapter one

A bag of dead fish

After 20 years of being employed by the police, out in the streets every day and dealing with challenging crimes, I was forced to start work in a boring, corporate coloured, lifeless police building. It was the type of building where every corridor was the same. Not just mundanely the same, but the type of corridors you would only see in your nightmares. Along these corridors, dazed police officers and civilian staff walked, often in such a trance they seemed unable to acknowledge mine or anybody else's existence.

It was a Thursday morning, and I followed my same old routine, walking through the car park, towards the police building, and past the emotionless officers. It seemed that every one of them had been conditioned throughout their life to be wishy-washy! I sighed... but somehow still made it through the station door.

Into the locker room I trudged, hundreds of grey characterless lockers lined up, numbered, but with no other signs of whom they belonged to. I opened my locker, locker 312, and inside was a photograph of my wife and children—a little reminder of the husband and father identity. I removed my clothes and put them on the floor, and in their place I began to put on my numbered uniform. Like a child on Halloween, I began to get dressed into my ill-fitting black military-style costume. Let's face it; a stretched, black lycra t-shirt doesn't do any favours for a forty-seven year-old who has developed a few lumps and bumps around his midriff. Luckily, I could hide my insecurities with a heavy bulletproof vest which instantly made me sweat. I squeezed on the belt which contained a baton, handcuffs and gas, then fastened it around my waist—the guise was almost complete.

I turned on the ironically named personal radio, which tuned me in, informing me straight away that the control room on their large electronic map were monitoring me. Big brother or big sister, sat on their big arses in the control room, would be watching me. They had me on their radar, and they would track me all day! A few thoughts passed through my mind, 'Why am I dressed like part of the Gestapo?' 'What happened to that trusted and proud British bobby I once was?' 'Surely, I am far too old to be pissing about playing army?'

The office I had been ordered to start work in was at the end of a corridor which would fit perfectly into a Scooby Doo cartoon. Like a condemned man walking the 'green mile,' I slowly walked towards my office and secretly hoped Scooby, Velma, and Shaggy would come running out of one of the doors to lighten my mood—but they never did. I turned my head to look at the first door I passed, and saw an emotionless face staring at me; I half expected him to shout 'dead man walking.' I smiled at him but immediately realised there would be no response. I couldn't find the strength to look through any more door holes.

Reaching the end of the corridor, I opened the key coded door and walked into the nest. Ambushed by the loud sound of bullshit, I looked to see other adults dressed in black army uniforms, desperately trying to appear busy. After observing them for a few minutes, I realised I had forgotten to collect my arrogant, egotistical, fake identity from my locker. I was new to this office and didn't know anybody who worked in there. Due to police cuts, the organisation had been dramatically reduced and some Hooray Henry working for the Government was paid huge amounts of money to restructure all the police practices, which had worked successfully for years. I had seen many changes, but this seemed to take the biscuit. Not being happy with restructuring the police, they also added years on the officers working career and reduced or 'stole' the officers' pensions.

The office was grim; the ceilings were low, everything felt compressed, just like the rooms in the new build houses. No natural light or fresh air entered the room, and the smell of bullshit lingered. I had for the last two years walked 10-15 miles a day on my beat and reduced crime dramatically. Not many officers walked the beat, and I needed to prove to myself this was the most successful way of policing and it was. However, having been forced into this new environment I was given a list of appointments which I had to complete. This meant even though I was dressed in my SS uniform, I would be spending most of my time in the station. The day began with an electronic briefing showing us the criminals who were active in the area I was employed to look after. I thought to myself, 'what's the point if we are stuck in the station all day?'

After this briefing, we sat at the computers, researching the appointments on our list, but before this; we needed to check our e-mails. The Inspector was in the next room, the Sergeant on the desk opposite me; everybody else just grabbed what computer they could get. Then there was a deadly, deadly silence, which was soon to be disrupted by the tap, tap, tap, tap, tap, tap, tapping of the keyboards. I logged into my e-mails. Tap, tap, tap, tap, tap....

PING—an e-mail notifying me that the station is being painted.

PING—a thought arrives in my head— 'What the fuck do I care?' Delete.

PING—an e-mail from my Sergeant— 'You can't take leave on that day because there is not enough staff to cover.'

PING—a thought arrives— 'What a nob, there will be loads of people just sat around on the days I want off.'

PING—an e-mail from a civilian— 'The Inspector says an officer has dropped out of doing nights this weekend, so he has told me, to tell you to do it.'

PING—a thought arrives— 'This will cock my weekend up, why could he not ask me himself? He is only twenty feet away and why is he asking a 17-year-old kid to do his dirty work? The slimy sod.'

PING—A morale-building e-mail arrives from the Superintendent, quoting Henry-the fucking-eighth. Delete, delete, delete! The taps on my keyboard are now becoming louder and angrier.

PING—An e-mail arrives from my Sergeant—'Officer, I have allocated this crime to you, a female has been in the pub this afternoon, and someone has stolen her bag of fresh fish. The fish has been returned to her, but it needs investigating.'

PING—A thought arrives in my head— 'Is this for real? You want me to investigate the theft of some pisshead's fish, which has been returned to her? And why are you sending me an e-mail? You're only sat across the desk from me.'

PING—Another e-mail arrives from my Sergeant who hasn't uttered a word and is still seated opposite me— 'Officer, I have received an e-mail from a police community support officer (PCSO), and they are going to e-mail you.'

PING—Another thought enters my skull— 'Oh shit.'

PING—An e-mail arrives from the PCSO—'Officer, the Sergeant, has asked me to contact you. I, along with another PCSO, have attended the pub in question, (trying to sound like a copper) and we have seized the CCTV, which shows two men stealing the bag of fish. He wants me to hand it over to you so the crime can be fully investigated and attempts can be done by you, to identify and arrest the men.'

PING—A thought arrives— 'Is this some exotic fish? Surely they don't need me to investigate the theft of a fucking dead fish, is this some piss-take?'

I hear voices in the corner of the room; I turn to see the Inspector talking to a few constables, who closely surround him trying to play the game. They were complaining and moaning about another officer not in the room. 'He should have done this; he should have done that.' I couldn't concentrate on my fish enquiry, and the complaining and negativity became louder and whinier. The combined voices churned around the room in a vibration; this vibration swirled around my mind, 'He should have, he should have, he should have, he should have, he should have, he should have!' Without any warning, my senses started to shut, my eyes lost focus, and the voices grew quieter and quieter, then from nowhere; tick, tick, tick, GNAB! The big bang in reverse: I felt nothing, I could see, but everything moved painfully slow, I could hardly hear anything and wondered what the hell had happened. It scared the shit out of me. Everything in my mind had been sucked into nothing, and although I was frightened, everything seemed peaceful.

A tear gathered in the corner of my eye, before crawling out and in slow motion, it trickled down my face—my mind had disappeared; I had been reduced to nothing. There was no personality, no ego. I shuffled into the Inspector's office and mumble to him, trying to tell him I needed to go home; he speaks, but I can't hear much, like being underwater in the swimming baths and listening to the voices on the surface. The conditioned mind tried to resurrect itself, just to be able to confirm to the Inspector I needed to go. It couldn't manage this simple task, so my body staggers out of the station.

For three months I sit in my garden, staring into space, with no contact from the outside world, wondering how after 47 years' life experience, all my mind could think about was a smelly, cold bag of dead fish, wrapped in a plastic bag and lying on the pub's sticky, carpeted floor.

Maybe it was a sign from God? Like the fish in the feeding of the five thousand and the fish was a message for me. Maybe the bag was the ego shell, and the fish were thoughts created by different identities which the mind had invented? Or maybe—I had just made the biggest mistake of my life and not realised what I had done.

Chapter two

A nice pleasant boy

*I was born simple-minded and with a bit of luck, I
will be simple-minded before the body passes.*

I appeared into the play of existence in the late
sixties and was raised within a working-class family,
in a working-class town, in the North of England.
People worked in the spinning mills, engineering
factories or down the coal mines. There were no
immediate signs of nature unless you looked for it,
but not many did, because to be honest—they
couldn't give two shits about it. Terraced houses,
factories, and large industrial chimneys lined the
streets, the air was dirty, and the constant rain made
everything seem so grim. The oil and soot appeared
to flow down the streets, and at night time, the dim
street lights hardly lit the pavement.

All this didn't concern the three year-old
Buddha, as he sat on the fluffy shag pile, stroking his
stubby fingers slowly through the soft carpet,
warmed by the groovy brown and yellow patterned
wallpaper and the hypnotising glow of the mini-
miser gas fire. The Buddha's eyes were transfixed on
the orange glow three feet in front of his gaze. His
focus couldn't even be distracted by the smell of fried
food wafting through the gaps around the closed

living room door or the sounds of the chitter-chatter created by his two devotees in an adjoining room. 'My Cherie amour, pretty little one that I adore,' played softly through the walls of the Buddha's meditation place. The living room door opens and the two devotees enter, holding with their offerings to the Buddha. 'Open your mouth,' one gently says. The Buddha straightens his fingers and presses his palms onto the shag pile carpet, before slowly opening his mouth. The devotee places their offering into his mouth.

'Mum, he won't eat all his fish fingers,' she shouts.

'What you doing, Sharon?' came the reply from the adjoining room.

'Feeding him—but he won't chew,' Sharon replied, almost in tears.

The Buddha's mother enters the room, shaking her head at Sharon, 'It's no wonder he's so fat and can't be bothered to walk or talk.'

Sharon was upset, 'what do you mean, Mum?'

'You and Tracy are spoiling him and making him lazy. Give me that food, I'll feed him.'

Although the Buddha didn't remove his gaze from the fire, he smiled from within as his mother lovingly fed him. Feeling full and content, the Buddha continued with his meditation. His mother and his devotees left the room and above the chanting of 'Que sera, sera whatever will be, will be the futures not ours to see, que sera, sera,' coming from the next room; he heard voices.

'Look, girls we need to start pushing your brother. He can't sit there for the rest of his life, who does that? Stop doing everything for him.'

The Buddha was happy and content as he meditated in front of the fire. He was in no danger and didn't feel the need to walk or talk. He had no interest in anything outside his meditation place. Why should he? Life was bliss! Over the next years he was escorted in and out of his special place to attend school, then in the final year of his primary school it started to happen......

There was a knock on our back door; 'Chris is here for you, don't have him stood out in the rain.' Funny, seeing as she had left him in the rain.

'Okay, coming, Mum.' I shouted, bounding downstairs two steps at a time.

Upon entering the kitchen, I saw my mother trying to sort the piles of washing into colours. I then saw Chris stood at the open back door in the pouring rain. My mother wasn't too keen on Chris and as I looked at his raincoat which was almost transparent with the rain, I could see why. In the front pouch of his coat, a packet of Embassy cigarettes could clearly be seen through his almost invisible coat, and seeing them smacked me in the face.

'Alright, Chris,' I said pointing at my own chest with my index finger and raising my eye brows, hoping that he would hide the cigarettes. Chris chuckled to himself covering the packet up with his hand, which made me chuckle.

'You two going to the match tonight?' my mother quizzed, still trying to sort out the washing piles.

'Yea, big match, it's gonna be good,' Chris replied trying to get on her good side, hoping that one day she would let him into her house.

'Okay, be careful, don't get into trouble.'

As I was walking out of the house my mother stopped me and spoke in a quiet voice, 'I hope you're not smoking.'

'I'm not, Mum, honest,' I replied with a cheeky grin, which always won my mother over.

'By the way, your school reports come back and it says you are a nice pleasant boy, but should try harder.'

'Try harder at what, Mum, being pleasanter?'

'Cheeky sod, you're eleven now, so you need to start working hard,' she said whilst laughing into her washing pile.

'Okay, see you later, Mum,' I said, pleased with myself for making her smile. I then walked off with Chris to begin our great adventure.

Once out of view of my house, Chris pulled out two cigarettes from his sodden packet and lit them up. We both puffed on the cigarettes, Chris put his arm around my shoulder and we both started to sing, 'Que Sera, Sera, whatever will be, will be, we're going to Wembley, Que Sera, Sera.'

'You got the tickets, Chris?' I asked, encouraging him to show me some proof.

'Course I have, my dad gave me two, here, I'll show you.' Chris threw his cigarette on the floor and pulled two tickets out of his jeans pocket. 'Look', he said, as he handed me one whilst grinning from ear to ear. I focused on the ticket: Bolton Wanderers v Everton, 1977, League cup semi-final, kick-off 7.30pm.

A big grin hit my face and we both sang, 'Que Sera, Sera, whatever will be, will be, we're going to Wembley, Que Sera, Sera,' before walking the short distance to the bus stop.

Waiting at the bus stop were the local Bolton Wanderers fans, including my eldest sister, Sharon; 'How have you two spunk bubbles got tickets?' she asked, trying to impress her friends who started slapping me and Chris about our heads.

'Get lost, it's nothing to do with you,' I replied.

'Well, keep out of my way, but get home safe, 'cos mum says I need to look after you.'

Chris pushed his shoulders back, 'Piss off, we don't need you to look after us, we've been going to the matches on our own for years.'

The slaps to our heads increased. 'Cheeky little skinhead twats,' shouted Big Dave, one of Sharon's hard-nut friends.

The double-decker bus arrived and all the fans pushed their way on-board, 'Stay downstairs you little bastards,' Sharon warned me and Chris.

'Go upstairs, James,' whispered Chris, whilst pushing me forwards.

'No, just stay downstairs or Dave will batter us.'

It didn't matter to me, because even whilst sitting downstairs we could still hear all the football chants; 'Wembley, Wembley, we're the famous Bolton Wanderers and we're going to Wembley. Wembley, Wembley.' The chants lasted all the way to Bolton bus station.

The passengers on our bus merged with the huge crowds flowing through the streets of Bolton, and the passing traffic illuminated them. 'Wanderers, Wanderers, Wanderers,' we all shouted as we made our way to the Lever Street railway bridge.

Once on the bridge, I froze, then placed both palms onto the mesh which prevented people from falling onto the railway lines. Mesmerised I pushed my face up to the mesh, staring at the four gigantic beams lighting up Burnden Park. The floodlights were a thousand times larger than the mini-miser gas fire in the Buddha's meditation room; I could have remained on the footbridge as the fans chanting and the waft of onions being fried at the burger vans flooded my senses.

'Come on, James, let's get a burger,' Chris shouted as he dragged me away from the wire mesh fence and snapping me back into personhood.

'I've not got any money, Chris.'

'I have,' Chris replied, laughing, as he pulled out a handful of five-pound notes from his pocket. 'The old bastard came in pissed again last night.'

Chris regularly stole from his dad's pockets and was responsible for his dad losing a job as a pub manager a few years later.

'I'm in heaven, Chris,' I told him as the onions and tomato sauce dripped down my chin.

Chris bought us both a match programme and the fresh print smelt nearly as good as the onions. My senses were exploding! The noise of fifty thousand human beings, the smell of the programme, the taste of the burgers and the sight of the floodlights coming closer, took my senses to cosmic levels. Could there be a more blissful feeling than this ultimate flow of consciousness?

Everton scored a goal in the first half, putting them through to the final. At the final whistle the atmosphere changed as thousands of Bolton fans angrily sang, 'you're gonna get your fucking heads kicked in!'

Myself and Chris walked back to the Lever Street railway bridge and as we crossed, I glanced back at the floodlights for a final time; the vibration of the crowd had changed to a low mumbling, the smells had disappeared and my awareness had returned to the level of an ordinary human being.

As we walked slowly towards the bus station, the mumbling of the Bolton fans was interrupted by a war cry; 'Everton! Everton!' At the opposite end of Thynne Street, near to the train station stood hundreds of Everton fans, who then started to charge like a herd of buffalos in our direction. Myself and Chris looked at each other without saying a word. My instinct told me we needed to find protection from adults. To my right I saw a grown man walking with the Bolton fans and holding his son's hand. His son looked to be about eight years-old, so I dragged Chris over towards them, hoping the gang of Everton fans would think we were with our dad and leave us alone.

The Everton fans charged through the Bolton fans punching and kicking them and all of a sudden three snarling buffalos appeared in front of the grown man I was stood with.

'Are you a Bolton bastard?' one asked, but before the man could reply, one of the Everton fans thrust a glass bottle into his face. Blood pumped from his face as he let go of his son's hand then fell to the ground. Other Everton fans kicked his head as he lay there unable to protect himself.

Upon witnessing this and without any warning, my senses started to shut, my eyes lost focus, and the chanting of the crowds grew quieter and quieter, then from nowhere; tick, tick, tick, BANG! The beginning, the big bang of the mind—this was where it all began, in these few moments everything appeared to happen in slow motion; my senses disappeared, no smells, no sounds, no blissful feeling anymore, everything was happening in the mind. I had the identity of a football fan who felt useless at being unable to help the grown man or his son, and weak because I wasn't strong enough to fight the Everton thugs.

After witnessing the glassing incident, myself and Chris ran away towards the bus station, being kicked and punched by the Everton fans as we ran. On the bus journey home, we didn't talk to each other about the assault, which replayed and was recorded inside my welcoming mind and I am sure Chris had his own story being recorded and re-played in his mind. As I tried to sleep that night a tear trickled down my face, as I thought of the young child screaming, as his whimpering father lay on the floor covered in blood. Little did I know; a tear wouldn't exit my eyes for another 36 years.

In this year I was also assaulted by members of the National Front whilst on a day out with my friends, I witnessed a sexual assault on a teenage girl by two teenage males, as well as a few more things an eleven-year-old child shouldn't see. To erase these incidents, I started sniffing Evo-stick glue which temporarily removed the images inside my mind. I have no doubt if heroin or crack cocaine would have been around, myself and my friends would have tried them.

I was fortunate to have had a good upbringing and until the glassing incident, the Buddha had been protected. Family holidays were to a caravan park in the Lake District, the freedom to run around in the fresh air made me feel so alive. I spent hours by the side of a river which ran through the caravan park. The cool breeze, the freshness of the river, and the aroma of the pine trees flowed through my nostrils and through my veins. Above the slow running river, midges skipped across the surface and the occasional fish rose to the surface then sank back, leaving widening rings on the water. My body was included in this ultimate dance of life, not apart from it. My father borrowed the caravan and borrowed a fishing rod from inside of it. We fished all week and eventually caught one rainbow trout, the first and last fish I ever caught. Something told me I should release the fish back into its natural environment, but the mind wanted to keep it as a trophy. My father whispered in my ear, 'You shouldn't keep the fish.' If only I had listened to this advice.

As there wasn't much to do at home, the majority of the kids hung around on street corners, like street rats. When it rained, as many of us as possible would huddle inside the red phone boxes; which were normally positioned outside pubs. The phone boxes had the ingrained odour of urine and cigarette smoke; each one of us would be spitting on the floor outside the phone box until you could see no more of it. One of us always had a cigarette which we passed around and when it came to the end of the cig—the game began.

The intention of the game was to prevent the ash from falling off. If it fell off and you were in possession of the cig, then you would be forced to eat the filter and whatever tobacco was left. I suppose it was like pass the parcel, but the ones who didn't win the prize got the treat instead, as they saw the loser of the game retch when they tried to swallow the cigarette stump. If you were the first in the phone box, you would squeeze into the left-hand corner, the unfortunate one would be crouched under the phone shelf, next to somebody's arse who was sat on the shelf. The very unfortunate ones, would pop their heads through a slight gap in the door, whilst the rest of their body got pissed wet through. If someone broke wind, there was no choice but to grin and bear it, or else you would lose your position inside the phone box.

Every now and again, a grown-up would stumble from the pub and kick us out of the phone box. This was the start of the next game, because as soon as he ended his call and turned to open the door; he would find himself trapped inside by a barricade—formed by the snotty kids who he had just kicked out. Every one of us was pissing ourselves, laughing at the grown-up who failed to budge the door and who's bawling and shouting couldn't be heard over all our laughing. After a few minutes, we calmed down and caught our breath; because we knew the next event was soon to take place—and this was life or death. As soon as everybody stopped laughing, we knew what to do next; we knew the exact moment to shout 'go, go, go,' and at that call, we would all starburst in every direction to escape from the angry drunk man trapped inside the phone box. They never caught us and looking back, probably accepted they had a part to play in the local kids' entertainment.

I find it bewildering seeing modern pictures of the red phone boxes in London, which people hang on their living room walls. I imagine people who buy these pictures think of Big Ben, Buckingham Palace, and the Queen—I think of booze, fag ends, spit, piss, puke and laughter. I never see any spit on the pavements within the pictures, or snotty-nosed kids having a fag.

In extremely cold weather we gathered on the pavement outside the cotton factory, and another huddle was formed in a factory door hole, our own ashram. We were warmed thoroughly by the heat, which was being leaked from the factory drying room; the pavements in front of the door hole were again covered in spit, chewing gum and fag ends. The size of the factories would make us feel so small, but at the same time, they would comfort us, because they belonged to us and we belonged to them. The gigantic chimneys were like our cannons, pointing up to the sky, ready to protect us from any imaginary invaders. We felt safe in this dreary but homely environment. Occasionally, a few of us would sneak into the cellar of the pub where Chris' dad worked, drinking stolen Newcastle brown ale and filling our hands with home-made tattoos.

When I was 15 years-old, the music industry was full of all kinds of identities: mods, rockers, punks, Ska, heavy metal—take your pick. Coming from a working-class town, the majority of my friends were into punk. However, the skinhead movement became very popular, mainly because of the Ska music, then along came 'Oi,' which was formed by right-wing skinhead groups or the Government, take your pick. My favourite song was by Blitz, 'Never surrender'. I even started a homemade tattoo on my arm with a sewing needle and Indian ink, which should have read 'skins never surrender'. However, I got bored, and it ended up reading 'skins never.' Surprisingly, this tattoo saved me in a tricky situation as an undercover cop, after a dealer asked me to show him my 'Tatts.' When I showed him my 'skins never' tattoo, he laughed and dealt me a bag of heroin.

The only thing I learned at school, was how to form spit bubbles on the end of my tongue, which I could, with a bit of extra training, blow into the air; I spent months mastering this skill. One of the favourite pastimes my friends took place in at school, was to spit on the wall, then bet another lad 50p to lick it off the wall!

After leaving school with no exams, my father got me a job working in an engineering factory. I went to work with 'real men' in an old factory. This building was in the next town to where I lived, and I landed lucky because I could get a lift off my dad. On-route, we collected Albert, an old man who looked about two hundred years- old; we also picked up Granville, who appeared to be my dad's age and stunk of booze every morning. Albert didn't speak much, but without fail, every morning, as soon as the factory came into our sight he spoke out loud, 'Once more into the breach,' which I later found out, was part of a poem about war, by Shakespeare; 'Once more unto the breach, dear friends, once more; or close the wall up with our English dead. In peace there's nothing so becomes a man, as modest stillness and humility: But when the blast of war blows in our ears, then imitate the action of the tiger...' Heavy, considering we were just going to work.

The biggest entertainment for the older workers, comprised of a 'who could fart the loudest' competition. The loudest fart award belonged to a chubby man, who shone with pride as his audience turned towards him, just after he had produced a fart that created a sound louder than the heavy machinery. 'Farting' was breaking wind, it used to be known as trumping or pumping. Another elderly chap called Malcolm, who ate prunes by the dozen, approached me occasionally, telling me that he had been for a crap and could only count 11 prune skins in the toilet when he knew he had eaten 12. Malcolm then turned around, to show me a prune skin which he had stuck to his shirt lap for entertainment value—I was learning so much. I went for everybody's butties and had to make the workers a brew. Obviously, they complained about their brew which didn't concern me as I expected this from the old buggers. The factory I was working in closed down, forcing us to travel to a new place of work near to Liverpool.

My welcome by the Scousers came from the shop-hand called Ian—amazingly, he really did only have one hand; his right hand ended with a stump just above his wrist. The vending machines were on the shop floor, in the centre of the factory and during a morning break as I waited for my coffee to arrive from one of the vending machines, my attention was drawn to a few office girls walking out of their office, onto the shop floor and in my direction. Never one to start conversations with the females, I thought 'here is my chance.' Turning to face the girls, I pushed my shoulders back, placed my hands onto my hips and I prepared myself to splutter some words in their direction—suddenly I felt something brushing the inside of my legs. I looked down to investigate the sensation and saw a massive stalker protruding from between my legs and pointing towards the girls. I turned around to see Ian crouching behind me laughing his head off, with his stumpy arm sticking out between my legs. I was so ashamed and embarrassed, I sneaked off to my machine whilst listening to Ian and the girls pissing themselves at myexpense. Ian was a lot of fun and helped me so much throughout the next nine years I worked at Liverpool.

After work I met Chris and other mates in the local pubs. The night's drinking normally ended up in street fights, which we saw as normal behaviour. However, things were getting out of hand, and I was in danger of getting into serious trouble. I honestly didn't believe I would live past thirty years of age or would end up in prison. As I was getting the wrong reputation, a lad from Manchester approached me, saying he had heard of me and asking if I wanted to run with a team of lads, committing armed robberies. He drove me to meet an older man, who was sitting outside a public house in the middle of Manchester;

this man just said hello and left it at that. He must have given me the okay because the lad kept pestering me after that meeting; I didn't want to become involved from the beginning, so I spent a lot of effort avoiding him, which seemed to work. I realise now what a lucky escape I had. Other lads from outer towns were coming to our pubs and bringing metal bars to attack us. The situation was getting very grim, worrying and scary; always wondering what was coming next, but then my guardian angel arrived.

Kath was a few years younger than I was and worked in the local cotton factory. Apart from being beautiful, she was a hard-case and spent a lot of her youth catching rats and rabbits with her older brother. Kath was always good for a laugh and after a lot of pestering, she agreed to start dating me.

The factories and pits were shutting down, Fred Dibnah was demolishing our protective chimneys; the community feeling in the working-class towns was disappearing, along with people's working-class identities. The humour was being replaced by bitterness and anger, but TV and drugs helped to keep the once proud communities sedated. The country had made use of the working class to make their empire great; now these people and their communities had been cast aside to make way for the so-called Information Age; if you didn't keep up, you were left behind.

I enjoyed my 10 years in the engineering factory, but as the Industrial Age came to a closure, I needed to move on, so I decided to join the police.

Chapter three

It's about time we got one in the police

I proposed to Kath in the pub and we agreed to get engaged, I then put the idea to her that we should wait 5 years' before we got married—which went down like a lead balloon. 'If I'm not good enough to marry now, you can fuck off,' Kath sharply replied to my suggestion.

It was now a case of stopping in a few nights and saving for a house—and the wedding. We spent many nights around Kath's house, eating meat and potato pie, which her mum had lovingly made. I worked overtime and Kath worked in the cotton mill during the week. Then on Saturdays, she worked in a shoe repairer shop.

The lads I grew up with were getting married, moving out of town with their jobs, going to prison, getting involved in drugs or becoming alcoholics. It was everybody's choice to do what they wanted to do, and it happened in a flash. Few of us kept in touch, there was no such thing as the internet or mobile phones, the only way to bump into each other was at the pub.

Our wedding day came closer, but there was a problem; me being Catholic and Kath Protestant. My dad's side of the family came from Southern Ireland, not too keen on the Protestants and Kath's family didn't trust the Irish. I went to a Catholic church and Kath belonged to the town's Parish church, a large impressive church. Both families wanted for us to get married in 'their' church. It tore Kath to bits, but she agreed to marry in the Catholic church, something I will never forget. She had to get her own back on the Irish, by naming our second daughter after the Queen—I'll give her that one.

It didn't seem fair, here we were, two kids who grew up in the same town, two working class kids; who just wanted to work and have fun. Then problems had been thrust upon us—in the name of religion. We never even thought about religion, but as soon as we wanted to show our love for each other by getting married, all the stereotypes and identities formed by religion hijacked us. We both visited the priest at the Catholic church and Kath told him straight away she wasn't changing her religion. The priest put her mind at ease by saying he suffered enough with his own parishioners, he didn't need her. We did a practise run of saying the vows in the church and whilst we were doing this, there was an open coffin, with a body inside it. This freaked Kath out, but we had a laugh about it and carried on with the plans for the big day. We had saved little so Kath's mum helped out with the reception meal and party. What money we had, was put down for a deposit on a two-up two-down terraced house. We lived there for twenty years until drug dealers, who had moved into the street, forced us out.

The wedding was fantastic and Kath looked amazing in the white wedding dress, which her mum had made for her. We booked a two-week bed-and-breakfast honeymoon in Greece, taking £100 spending money between us, for the whole two weeks. It was a great honeymoon, even though we only had enough cash for one drink of beer every day and I spent three days' beer money on yogurt which I had to spread over my sunburn, to cool me down. We returned from Greece and set about decorating our new home and getting ready for our married life together.

Some people at the factory I worked in lost their jobs through redundancy and I could sense that the engineering industry was on its arse. The Industrial Age was coming to an end, so for security reasons, I decided to look for another job. At first, I thought of being a fireman; but even as a young child I was scared of heights, so I gave this a miss. Then, after speaking to a neighbour who told me he was retiring as a police officer, I decided to apply for the cops. The fact that I was applying to be a police officer surprised all my friends and family. I can't describe why I wanted to join the police, it was probably because this was the only job I could think of which would offer security for my family and was a profession which I didn't need qualifications for. The only requirement to join the police was to have life experience, so I qualified. Apart from watching The Bill, which was a Metropolitan police TV programme,

I didn't know about Government politics, how they controlled the country or the police force's role.

When I applied to join the police force, my understanding was that I would get paid to protect life and property—this seemed appealing. The brochure sent by the police during the application process showed officers walking the beat, talking to people and even cycling through an idyllic English village. I thought to myself 'is there such a place as beautiful as this?'—because I had never seen such a gorgeous setting before in my life. Today, police don't walk their areas or talk to the public, something sadly missing in the role of a police officer. The traditional way of policing does and can work; in my final years in the police I walked every day as a neighbourhood officer, reducing crime, whilst every other officer felt the need to drive everywhere and have as little contact with the public as possible. It has been months since I have seen police driving around, more worryingly; it has been years since I saw a police officer walking his or her beat. Little did I know, that the police force I joined, would eventually turn into a service, who would bow down to every kind of minor public complaint and be so answerable to every little whim. I also blame the public for this; who probably wouldn't even make a complaint if they had to get off their arses and walk to a phone box. The change in how the police are managed, prevents the officers spending their time protecting the most vulnerable members of society. The morale of the officers has been destroyed by the Government's neglect. A

Government who seem to have their own plans and the police aren't part of these plans.

I applied for the police just after I married and reached the final interview; only to be told that they could not accept me because I had tattoos on my hand—fucking Chris! Even though I was skint, I paid to have the tattoos removed and re-applied, this time minus tattoos I passed the interview and the police gave me a starting date. Kath had real problems giving birth to our first daughter and as a result, she could not return to work in the factory and couldn't claim any benefits, so we had to rely on my wage which was a serious worry, as we had more outgoings than incomings. The police pay was not much better than what I was earning in engineering, but we stayed afloat with the help of a few loans.

I wasn't prepared or warned that by joining the police, my social life might suffer. Most people watch TV programmes and believe the police force is fantastic for a social life, but because of a variety of reasons, I found out that this was untrue. Many of my friends from my hometown turned their backs on me as they knew nobody who joined the police and now felt they had to be very careful in what they said or did. This was clear if I went out to the local pubs, when comments such as 'Watch what you say, there's a copper here' or 'be careful, he will lock you up,' would be spoken loud enough so I could hear. Although some of these comments may have been said half-jokingly, people would introduce me to each other as a 'copper' and any conversations ended up discussing the police. I realised that as soon as this was done, people stopped being themselves around me. My close friend Chris moved to a different town with his father and we eventually lost touch with each other.

My relatives had strong connections with Southern Ireland and on one family occasion; an aunty shouted in front of everyone: 'It's about time we got one in the police,' as though I had infiltrated them. Many 2nd and 3rd generation Irish still try to cling on to the fairy tale of being Irish, this is clear to see in America. But because of the bombings committed by the IRA in England, my father warned me it would be wise to keep my mouth shut about having any link to being Irish. Ireland wasn't mentioned in the family home during my childhood and I never had any reason to be interested in the country, anyway. It was only when I had children and looked back at my family tree I understood the Irish side of my family's history. To research my heritage and the country where I could have been born would have been interesting, but three things made this impossible: I was an English traitor, I was a policeman working for the Queen, and I had married a Protestant. Just three things, which I don't think would have gone down well with the Irish Republican Army if I was ever to go back and reclaim my Irish heritage.

Later on in life when I was working undercover, I attempted to find a belonging to Ireland. I learned how to play the tin whistle and could play a few Republican tunes. I visited my grandparents' cottage in Southern Ireland, but because it was so hard to keep my identity as a policeman and my wife's religion a secret, it was more trouble than it was worth and I realised that it would be uncomfortable returning. This is frustrating because I admire their pride and unity. Similar scenarios are happening within the Asian communities in England but their links to their parents' countries are stronger, as they find it harder to keep it a secret. I suppose, we should all be grateful, for England letting our grandparents in. Even though their children and grandchildren lost all real connection with their home countries and will never feel connected.

I feel I have been so lucky to marry Kath, who has nothing at all to do with the police. It is strange to see, but as soon as most people become employed by the police service, their perspective on life and their perspective on people who are not employed in their profession, changes. Many, many police officers turn to each other and people would be amazed to find out how many form relationships, get married, even get divorced from their partners to marry a police officer of their choice. This is probably why the divorce statistics are so high in the police. I have seen married officers working the same shift, dealing with the same incidents and often wonder what the hell they talk about when they finish their shifts and go home. I have only attended one or two police nights out in the last fifteen years. These social events are known as 'police do's' and self-importance, arrogance and alcohol combined results in a dangerous situation. Many nights out end up with the police causing trouble, sometimes with each other, but mostly with normal members of the public. The last night I went out with the police, it ended up with one officer making a smart comment to a civilian, everything erupted, which ended up with another officer being stabbed in his stomach. I vowed never to attend another 'police do'. This incident didn't help my mental state, because at the time of this incident, unbeknown to myself I was already suffering from post-traumatic stress and already distancing myself away from the rest of the world.

During my successful interview to get into the police, I found it to be more relaxed than in my previous final interview, which took place a few years earlier. Times had changed, in 1990 the interview board were in full uniform (including hat), sat behind a desk and guided me to sit on a chair in front of their desk. The chair was lower than the desk to make me feel inferior as I had to look up towards the interviewing officers. It didn't matter really because they had spotted the tattoos on my hand. The successful interview was relaxing because the officers who interviewed me wore civilian clothing and we sat around in a nice friendly circle—on similar sized chairs. I felt more at ease during this interview and although the main interviewer said I was not as articulate as the other candidates; they had agreed to give me a job in the police. They then asked if I had any preferences to where I wanted to work, so I named the inner city just outside Manchester which my neighbour had suggested. They rubbed their hands, smiled and said that would be just fine.

I didn't know what happened in this city, but my neighbour who had advised me to join the police, told me to ask for this area. 'You will learn more there in five years, than you will in thirty years in other areas,' he told me. This city is a place where most of the northern armed robbers serve their apprenticeship. It also prided itself with a gang structure so solid they would have put any other gang to shame throughout the country.

Before I could go to the police station where they had posted me to, I had basic training to complete and also needed to be measured up for my uniform. I attended the police training centre as directed by my joining letter then sat around inside a room full of people from every walk of life—the chosen ones—who had been selected to join the police family. The chosen ones now needed to be very careful about what they said and how they acted because their every movement would now be scrutinised.

The training staff arrived; full of optimism and full of their self-importance. They were in control of a new batch of human beings, who they had to form into what the police force expected of a British bobby. It wasn't until later in my career when I realised that these trainers were better spoken and educated than the majority of other police officers and they had the wisdom of being able to get away from front line policing, by finding a role within the training school. In the school, they could still fuel their police egos, even though they were being employed as more of a conditioner than a police officer. They didn't work nights and although they had escaped the hard job of a real front line police officer, they were better thought of by the superior officers. I didn't have much in common with the recruits and the ones who I had something in common with kept it to themselves. I had worked for ten years in the factory, been married and had a daughter. I probably had more life experience than a lot of the probationers but this was now my chosen profession and I needed to put up with all the bullshit if I wanted to keep hold of this job. After going home from work, covered in oil and completely knackered, I was now going home after nodding and smiling at the tutor constables and sitting around in a classroom.

The training officers gave us a personal development profile (PDP) to fill in and this had to be completed over a two-year period. If you completed everything within the PDP and after two years you were a competent officer, the trainee would become a real police officer, not a probationer. Nobody wanted to be a probationer as this was the lowest of the low in the police 'family.' The probationers were commonly known as 'sprogs' when they eventually reached their nominated police station. The PDP was intended as a diagnostic tool to identify skills and abilities, of which there were 36 named ones. Surprisingly, being yourself wasn't one of them? The 36 skills and abilities were evidenced through self -assessments and tutorials; conducted by experienced officers. After the tutorials, the trainee would be given an action plan to maintain their strengths and improve their weaknesses. The 36 skills and abilities were grouped under the headings: Desired character traits, monitoring personal performance, communication and relationships with others, investigation, knowledge, decision making, problem solving and planning, practical effectiveness and written reports.

At the beginning, it was embarrassing for a 27-year-old married man, because the only comments I could make up were 'I need to improve on polishing my shoes' or 'I need to concentrate more.' In my youth I attended confession at church and I had to make something bad up to tell the priest, just to break the silence. The confessions also took place at secondary school where the kids went into the confession box and from behind the screen; they informed him they had murdered somebody. It was complete bollocks because even if you really had done something terrible, your only punishment was to say ten hail Marys and ten Our fathers; then all our sins were forgiven. I half-expected that the training staff were going to give us prayers, to punish us for our failings.

Because I had never concentrated at school, I found the classroom-based teaching difficult, and I therefore needed to put in extra hours at home to make sure I passed the tests. The other training which the trainers gave to us was in the form of roleplays. During the roleplays, probationers in uniform would act out and deal with scenarios, which were acted out by other probationers wearing their own clothes and pretending to be members of the public. Although some of the role plays were funny, I found the whole thing cringe-worthy; the acting and pretending it was all real was hard to take in. I got put on a development plan by the tutors for taking the piss out of other officers, but what did they expect? I had worked at a factory in Liverpool for nine years, where if you didn't take the piss, there was something wrong. So I bit my tongue and started being more supportive to the officers to pass my action plan; at least I now had something to be action planned for.

As if the 36 skills and abilities weren't enough to grasp, probationers during their first two years were also expected to perform the following 39 tasks to a competent level of performance: using radio, answering the telephone, document/books, pocket notebook entries, statement taking, dealing with property, attending the scene of a crime, making an arrest, reporting offenders, executing warrants, serving summons, stopping motor vehicles, administrating first aid, talking to offender/victim/witness, delivering a message, preparation of a file, attending the scene of an accident, preparing a sketch plan, preserving evidence, public order, searching people/vehicle/premises, using staff/cuffs/shield, using breath test devices, giving evidence, gaoler, non-offence encounters, seeking advice, checking premises, examination of documents, ejecting people, sudden deaths, handling dangerous objects and domestic disputes.

After three months of training in a safe environment, the probationers were released to start at the stations which they had been posted to. Here the probationers could tick off the 39 tasks to prove they were competent and could pass their probation. The game had begun. It was a game, and it was an identity, because being a police officer is just a role, which they didn't explain to us. It hit home years later when I worked undercover buying Class A drugs. I needed to create another identity and another role to become accepted on the street as a heroin addict, like I had to fit in to become a police officer. Only this time after being accepted as a heroin addict I needed to leave the role after each deployment then adapt to being a police officer, and after returning home I was the loving father and husband. Because of these identities and roles, I didn't know who the real 'I' was. It was a game, an illusion, a fantasy and a situation which finally woke me up.

I managed to get hold of a mini metro motor vehicle, which to be honest was held together with elastic bands. The winter was approaching, our house was not decorated, and it didn't have any heating, apart from a 3-bar gas fire in the living room. Saying goodbye to my wife and daughter, I made the fifteen-mile journey to the station where I had been posted. Because of our financial difficulties, I put two pounds' worth of petrol into the car, and hoped for the best. I knew I had a challenge ahead of me but didn't realise how big the challenge was going to be.

On the first day, I drove into the city and as I did, the sight of the large tower blocks seemed so intimidating, the natural environment comprised of the odd tree dotted about amongst all the surrounding concrete. I hadn't been to a city before and it shocked me how large and how ugly it was. Joy Divisions 'New Dawn Fades' played on my car radio and complimented this city to a tee—it still does. If I thought my home industrial town was grim, this place took the biscuit. There was little nature to be seen apart from the dirty trees which appeared to have broken through the cracked pavements and were surrounded by dog shit which the shuffling, stooped pedestrians side-stepped to avoid mucking up their only pair of shoes. This place made my chest tighten. The atmosphere made me instantly miserable; my mind cast itself back to seeing the police brochure, and the village police officer cycling in the beautiful village surrounding as I thought 'why do you keep ending up in shitholes?' As I approached the police station, I reminded myself that this was the job and place I'd chosen, so I had no choice but to get on with it.

As I pulled into the rear car park of the station and passed the marked police vehicles, a thought popped into my head; 'How the fuck have you become a policeman?' I shrugged my shoulders before collecting my uniform from inside a cardboard box in the boot of my car. Anxiously I walked towards the large Victorian built station and had the same feeling that a person would have when they go to prison for the first time. Fresh out of the box, I would be their bitch; it didn't matter if I was 27 years-old, married with a daughter: I would still be their bitch. I wasn't sure where to go, so I followed the other people entering the large heavy doors, which allowed entry into the building. Upon entering, I noticed a long corridor which lead to the front of the building. Along this corridor were two sets of heavy doors which had glass panels in them. The character of the building hit me; it gave me the feeling that the ghosts of a thousand coppers had passed through the building before me and they were still walking along the corridors, a sense which doesn't exist in the modern corporate police buildings.

To my left, immediately after entering the building were the doors to the male locker room. In this room, several bobbies stood in a huddle, putting their uniforms on, smoking and laughing amongst themselves. I wanted to talk to the officers in the locker room, but seeing as I hadn't been allocated a locker yet, I thought it would have been weird if I entered the locker room without a reason. So I continued to shuffle down the corridor carrying my uniform, hoping I would bump into someone who could help this desperate new bobby. At the end of the corridor I came across a small room; in this room sat two police officers behind a desk. I looked at their shoulders and saw three stripes, which meant they were Sergeants, who were in charge of constables. With a stutter I explained who I was, and with a smirk they told me to drop my box off in the next room to theirs, then get ready for parade. I didn't know what getting ready for parade was, so I put on everything I had been issued with, a helmet, white shirt, black trousers, tie and a wooden truncheon, which slipped down a long pocket in the side of my trousers, and my handcuffs. I also carried my torch, an odd thing to do, because it was 6.45 am and daylight outside.

I walked into the parade room and what an idiot I felt. My shift sat around a group of four desks, which they'd pushed together to make one larger one. Most of them were smoking and looked as though they had just finished their shift; not starting it! A couple of cops looked in my direction but didn't appear to take much notice so I positioned myself at the back of the room; many cops do this when they are on a night out so they can see everybody around them. Whilst I leant against the wall I observed a young fresh officer who must have been about 20 years-old. This officer supplied the others with cups of coffee and tea then handed radios to them. The young officer glanced in my direction and seemed to be thinking 'thank fuck there's somebody else I can hand over all this shit over to.' I should have helped him, but my father had always advised me not to volunteer for anything, so I didn't. The tasks would be coming my way eventually, anyway. I was handed a radio and needed to ask an officer at the side of me how to switch it on. Once it was switched on, I heard a strange language; it was police jargon which had been developed over centuries and a language only known to the police. A language I realised when working undercover could give you away as being a cop. The double doors to the room swung open and in entered a large 'roly-poly' cop—the Inspector of our shift. An Inspector is one step-up the ranking from a Sergeant, and more often than not, stayed in their offices. The mood changed and all the officers jumped to their feet then placed their helmets on their heads. They held out their handcuffs in one hand and wooden truncheon in the other hand; this was showing your appointments. Something made me laugh inside: the size of the policewomen's truncheon. They were tiny and the policewomen always looked embarrassed to produce these vibrator sized weapons. I fumbled about and made a half attempted effort to produce my appointments. The Inspector sat at the head of the desks, like your father would have done at meal time. Then just like Meatloaf in concert, he then dabbed the sweat from his forehead with a handkerchief. He then informed officers of their daily duties; the van crew never changed, and comprised of the two most experienced bobbies on the shift. I later found out that the two who made up our van crew were the laziest bastards you could imagine. They never put pen to paper and always 'backed up' other officers to jobs, never getting to the incident first. I wasn't even mentioned in the duties until the regular duties were given out. After these had been dished out, one officer remained without a partner. The Inspector said to this officer, 'Paul you take the sprog out.' Paul whispered 'For fucks sake' under his breath. I don't know what was worse; the fact that the Inspector never even looked at me and referred to me as a sprog, or that Paul was only two feet away from me and knew I could hear his disappointment. The other officers turned to Paul and laughed.

Paul seemed a nice bloke though, probably too nice to be a cop and he retired with not much service. He told me what equipment I needed to take to the van, and we walked off down the corridor. I couldn't believe it, a real cop in a van, dealing with real problems. None of the role play shit, this was reality and little did I know what a fucked up, dangerous place it would turn out to be.

Paul's first comment surprised me; 'don't be seen speaking to the supervision, everybody will think you're a grass.' I'd heard the criminals in the city were proud of the fact they weren't grasses, but I never expected it within the cops. I'm sure this was unique to this inner city station, because when I later moved to a station outside the city, I couldn't believe how much constables sucked up to their supervisors and took pleasure by dropping you in the shit. After getting into the van, Paul didn't speak much so I tried to start conversation, but after a while I got the feeling I had been getting on his nerves, so I kept quiet. Ready for action I became giddy as we left the station car park. Paul drove the van to a nearby public park, he pulled up next to the park's only bushes, turned off the engine, closed his eyes and went to fucking sleep! It was 07.15am and I sat there for an hour listening to his snoring. I tried to look busy, by shuffling paperwork about, just in case a member of the public walked past, and my body ached with energy. After waking up, he drove out of the park and drove towards an industrial site. I wondered if he had anything exciting lined up for me; not to disappoint, he pulled up opposite a breakfast cabin. We both got out and ordered an egg and bacon butty, before getting back into the van and then spent another hour watching the traffic going past and eating our breakfast. The roleplays at training school hadn't prepared me for this kind of action; they also hadn't prepared me for the real action that I would be facing in years to come. If I would have known what was ahead of me, I may have enjoyed every second sat in the van with Paul, chilling out. Most early shifts were like this and the radio didn't really get busy until about 1pm. It took me a while to realize it, but this was the time when most criminals got out of bed to start their thieving or as they put it, grafting.

The chilling out period only lasted a few weeks as police officers had started to be monitored by performance indicators. Each officer and each shift were monitored; by how many arrests they made, how many parking tickets/producers they gave out, how many people they stopped and searched and numerous other ways of checking what officers were doing during their shift. These actions would be named a 'tick in the book' and the favourite and probably easiest tick was the producer. An officer would stop a motorist then hand them a ticket, giving them the chance to produce their documents at a police station within seven days. If the documents weren't produced, the officer would report the motorists for document offences—another tick in the book. Performance indicators didn't do much for public relations. One morning an officer playing the performance indicator game stopped 40 motorists and handed them a producer. The motorists were on their way to work, so if the public didn't hate the police beforehand they did after that. The supervision being monitored for the first time in their careers didn't care, they just said; 'well if he can do it, why can't you?'

After the first few weeks, I was handed over the brew making duties and responsibility for handing out the radios. I started to build up some paperwork for reporting motorists, as well as reports for traffic accidents and prisoner files. So I went to work an hour early without pay, so I could check my paperwork and make a brew for all the ungrateful bobbies, who never seemed to have any paperwork to do. The time spent in a van was short lived, because the more experienced cops were given this luxury. I spent the next six months walking alone around the shithole which I had somehow found myself policing. Nights were gruelling, as there were no shops and all the pubs had been burned down for not paying protection money. I ended up walking around terraced streets, in the middle of winter, bored shitless. The only good thing about winter was that when it snowed it covered all the grimy, shitty streets up. I was still being monitored by performance indicators and because I couldn't get around I ended scraping ice off parked vehicles window screens, to see if their tax disc was in date. Very grim.

Every now and again a call came over the radio: 'Is the sprog free?' When I heard this request, my heart sank. This happened during my first night shift: 'Is the sprog free? We have two males detained.' I confirmed I was free and the control room dispatched an officer to pick me up. This officer conveyed me to the other side of town and upon reaching the location I saw two young lads lying on the floor next to the van belonging to the van-crew. Upon closer inspection I noticed the lads were covered in blood; one of the van-crew told me they had caught the lads breaking into a vehicle and as they tried to arrest them, the young lads had started fighting which is why they were now injured.

'Right' said the officer, 'book one in under my name and one under his,' pointing towards his mate.

With the help of my driver I took these two lads into the police station, interviewed them both and completed the paper file to send them to court. I also had to explain to their solicitors how their faces had ended mashed up. The van-crew did nothing at all, but both officers got a tick in the book. Commonly known as 'cuffing a job' or 'twirling,' this could be anything from taking details from victims of crime and not doing anything about it, or handing your shit over to another officer who then had to deal with it, I found it easier to just get on with it myself. A lot of officers spent more time and effort cuffing or twirling jobs than they spent dealing with jobs. The most common job a probationer was 'twirled' with was what other officers called a 'ball of shit.' A ball of shit was any job or investigation with many, many complex lines of enquiry which an officer would have picked up and found too problematic to complete. The officers who wanted to be supervisors would say it wasn't a ball of shit, it was a challenge, but I didn't see many of them taking on this so-called challenge.

Being a sprog, accepting a ball of shit was the same as making the brews or handing the radios out—you had to do it or the officers on your shift would have nothing to do with you. It would all be justified as gaining valuable experience when it was just the experienced officers being bone-idle bastards. Most of the probationers' prisoners in their early days would have been given to them. Although it was good to gain knowledge, to catch your own criminals was something the probationers joined the police to do. As soon as they gained enough confidence using the system and about the area where they worked, this was something most probationers strived to do—at least you would now only be dealing with your own shit. After putting up with all the crap for two years and gaining a lot of 'valuable' experience from all the incidents I dealt with, I passed all the criteria and completed the 39 tasks to become a fully-fledged police officer. No longer a sprog, I could take some interest in other aspects of policing.

Chapter four

Has anybody tried talking to these children?

PHEW! No longer a sprog, I felt like an adult once again. I had been blessed with another daughter and was still living in my two-up two-down terraced house, still with no heating and little furniture. My wife got a job delivering parcels, so she labelled the parcels during the day and then after or before my shift in the police, we drove around with our two daughters, in the mini metro, trying to get rid of the parcels. I think she got about ten pence for every parcel she delivered. It always amazed me, that in the so-called rougher areas, the neighbours took the parcels in if the occupants weren't home. But as soon as we went on the posh estates, around 50% of the residents didn't even speak to their neighbours, and refused to take the parcel.

We had holidays by getting loans from the police credit union and we also re mortgaged our house to pay for repairs to the structure of it, and to cover general day-to-day expenses. The beauty and love I felt from my wife and daughters made it all worthwhile and no matter how hard it was, the feeling of having a close family surrounding me made me feel special and lucky. If I had been working nights, I would wake up to find all my wife's friends along with their children, filling our house, chatting away and having brews. I loved this atmosphere and the wage I brought in from the police gave us security to bring our family up without too many worries. We were never going to be Rothschilds, but felt happy with our lot. I was enjoying working in the police and became a confident police officer. The shift I was part of turned out to be friendly and sometimes after work we went for a beer together in the station bar.

As my house was just off the area where I worked, occasionally, I drove home in my lunchtime to show my children the police van and all the flashing lights. This was before the communication room tracked our every single move. I was proud to be a police office and little actions like showing my wife and children the van helped them to feel involved in my job. I'm afraid this would no longer be possible because the communication room or a supervisor would sit at their desks tracking officers' radios and would find great pleasure in disciplining them for going home in the van. I was now one of the lucky ones, driving a van around to jobs and new probationers were coming through on my shift to walk the streets. Naturally, they should have been making the brews and dishing out the radios, however times were changing and new probationers were being encouraged to challenge these demeaning duties, after a while they even stopped walking the beat. This resulted in each officer making their own brews and booking out their own radio because the new probationers refused to do it; the probationers would be encouraged to take a grievance out against anybody who tried to make them do something which they deemed wasn't acceptable. I didn't mind, because I knew how bad it was to be treated like shit, but some of the more experienced officers found it hard to come to terms with.

During a night shift, an experienced officer arrested a male for being drunk and disorderly and as usual, he shouted up for the sprog to deal with the drunk. The probationer was collected and transported to meet the experienced officer who told him he would be dealing with the prisoner. I was already in the custody office dealing with my own prisoner when I noticed the red-faced experienced officer, the probationer and their 'prisoner' enter the custody office. Upon entering, the custody Sergeant asked the constables why the prisoner had been detained. The experienced bobby, expecting the probationer to tell the Sergeant that the male had been arrested for drunk and disorderly, looked shocked when he didn't speak a word.

'Well?' bellowed the Sergeant, 'Is somebody going to tell me?' The anger of the Sergeant got everybody's attention.

The experienced bobby, whose face was getting redder and redder, looked angrily at the probationer saying; 'Well, tell the Sergeant he has been arrested for being drunk and disorderly.'

With baited breath, everybody in the custody office was now looking for the reply. The probationer said: 'But he wasn't disorderly, Sergeant, so I didn't arrest him.'

'What!' this was unheard of. The experienced officer turned to the probationer and shouted; 'fuck off you workshy bastard, I'll deal with him!'

The probationer walked out of the custody office and the red-faced bobby dealt with the prisoner. This was a sign of things to come, there would be no more shouting the sprog up to deal with shitty jobs. Nobody spoke about this incident throughout the remainder of the shift, but the following day the Sergeant called every officer into his office one by one, and asked us our thoughts on the probationer, if he could be trusted and if he worked hard? I couldn't believe this! the police system clamped down on the probationer because he spoke up for himself. I said he worked hard, so the Sergeant wrote it down on a list; I looked at the list and noticed that a few officers on my shift said he was lazy. The officer struggled throughout his probation and eventually moved areas.

I didn't mind working with the probationers and tutored a few. The older cops still treated them like shit though, which wasn't productive at all. As I had put on a few pounds from being sat in a van and eating my children's leftover meals, I trained with a probationer, a martial arts expert, to get fitter. He used me as a human punch bag, but it made me sweat and the pounds were disappearing. One shift I partnered up with Bruce Lee and as we drove along the street, we noticed two grown men fighting on the pavement opposite one of the toughest pubs in the city. Even though it was common to see such behaviour we couldn't be seen to ignore it. Myself and Bruce got out of the van or if you want the police terminology, we 'alighted from our vehicle.' We had sorted out lots of fights, so this wasn't going to be a problem, or so we thought.

I walked up to the men and tried the usual calm approach of 'come on lads, break it up.'

'Fuck off, Dibble, what the fuck has it got to do with you?' came the reply. (Officer Dibble was a cartoon character in the cartoon 'Top Cat'.)

A reasonable question I thought, but as an officer of the peace, I couldn't allow these men to fight and swear in the street and I didn't really want to spend much time trying to explain my involvement in their entertainment. So I asked them to break it up once more.

'Come near me and I'll break your neck,' one of them replied.

I felt as though I wasn't getting through to these men, so I handcuffed one and Bruce handcuffed the other. Not being the most passive human beings, the men started to perform by struggling, screaming and shouting at us, which didn't make the task easy and we all ended up rolling about on the floor.

Out of the grunting and shouting I heard a shout; 'Oi, you black bastards, what are you doing to them?'

Black bastards was yet another pet name for police officers. I knew it wasn't the two men we were trying to arrest shouting these comments, so I looked up and across the road I saw twenty to thirty Neanderthals stood outside the pub. This group wore thick gold chains around their necks and gold teeth in their mouths provided by the NHS. They were the city's criminal elite.

Myself and Bruce looked at each other and thought 'oh fuck' as the men ran across the road to release their friends. I wasn't concerned about losing the prisoner but I couldn't lose my handcuffs or else I would be disciplined, so I gripped them as hard as I could, even though the prisoners' 'friends' punched, kicked and tried to drag their mates away from us. We kept a few away by swinging our truncheons and kicking out, but they weren't backing off. Bruce shouted up for backup on his radio, but wasn't heard because we had stopped in a location which didn't have great radio reception. Luckily after about five minutes, a lone officer drove past and as soon as he switched on the van's blue lights, the 'friends' of the prisoners ran away; they must have thought the police van contained lots of cops. I unfolded my fingers, which had been welded to my handcuffs and threw the prisoner in the back of my van. Myself and Bruce sat in our van and started to laugh as we had been so lucky; apart from a few cuts and bruises we were still alive and had kept hold of our prisoners and handcuffs. The newly issued body armour we wore uncomfortably under our shirt and tie saved us both from receiving several broken ribs. When we got back to the station our Sergeant asked why we hadn't shouted up for help. Bruce did shout up, but our radios were on trial in the city and the supervisors were noting which locations in the city the new radios were not getting reception, and quite a few areas provided little or no reception. To be fair, the radios needed to be improved and these new radios had been designed so they couldn't be scanned by criminals, but this came at a cost sometimes; especially until the reception difficulties were ironed out.

The criminals purchased scanners, equipment sold publicly, to listen into police radio channels—useful to the criminals if they committed armed robberies or if being chased in stolen vehicles. Somehow, they got hold of equipment which allowed them to talk over our channels and throughout December they played Christmas songs over the airwaves or shouted obscenities. Even though the criminals lifted our Christmas spirits, the blockage of the airwaves proved to be a pain in the arse and dangerous to officers on the street. On one occasion, I attended a burglary at a Chinese chip shop and because the owners of the shop couldn't speak English, I shouted the telephone number of the shop over my radio and asked the communications room to ask an interpreter to phone the shop's telephone number. Within seconds the shop's number rang and the owner picked it up.

'What great service' I thought to myself, but upon answering the call the shopkeeper looked shocked and handed the phone to me.

'Hello,' I asked expecting to speak to an interpreter 'Is there a problem?'

It stunned me when the caller replied; 'Yes there is a fucking problem, I've told him to get his fucking grassing Chinese arse out of the country, or I will burn his shop down.'

It was impossible to trace the person responsible and I tried to explain to the shopkeeper what had just happened and there was little I could do about it. The criminals were monitoring us, and had stolen or bought a few police radios from somewhere. The officer conversations were kept to a minimum, but this didn't stop several of the city's criminals turning up to jobs before us, to see what had happened and who had been grassing.

The supervisors higher up the chain of command heard about the incident involving myself and Bruce and realised that if we had been seriously injured, somebody would have been in the shit. A mistake had been made and to make sure the radios were not withdrawn from the streets; myself and Bruce both got recommended for an award from the Chief Constable, the highest-ranking police officer. Maybe they thought we really deserved it? I'll never know. Our injuries were never recorded in the injury on duty book because this wasn't encouraged at the time. Everybody seemed happy: my wife and I met the Chief Constable who gave me a commendation certificate at an awards ceremony. I had a write-up in my local paper which boosted my ego and I knew it would help me get into squads in the future. The supervisor who put me up for the award could, if he went for further promotion, use this as an example of supporting his officers. The higher-ranking officers were happy, because there was no complaint about the radios or the injuries and the radio company were happy because there was no complaint from the police, which could have prevented them making lots of money. The police force was happy because they had the opportunity to show the public how brave their officers were. In the meantime, my prisoner received a 50 pound fine at court. This was how one small incident could unfold, although at the time I didn't realise why.

Now in charge of a vehicle I got about easier and became more involved in the performance indicator game; with the keys to a van I now stopped cars racing around the streets. Chasing stolen cars happened every day, because in the nineties the cars were so easy to break into. What interested me mainly was the gang structure or what they now call an 'OCG, organised crime group.' An intelligence officer called Fred who I had the upmost respect for took it upon himself to research the gang structure of this city and produced a chart which showed photographs of the gang members; it also displayed the rank structure. The gang included over 100 serious criminals, who may be called on to commit criminal activities. Any of the 100 members could have gone into the outer surrounding towns and took them over if they had been allowed.

I first looked at the gang chart and recognised none of the faces on the photographs. I made it my business to know every one of the gang throughout the following years and wanted to know every move they made. Whilst some officers stopped single females going to work just so they could hand them a producer and top up their performance indicator figures, I preferred to drive around the shitty areas and stop all the gang members, so I could tick them off my mental gang chart. The gang members would be straight in my face, shouting my collar number out aloud, claiming I was harassing them and said they would complain about me. They spouted all the usual comments to break the officer who had the 'nerve' to stop them. This was intimidating at first and why many cops didn't get involved with the gangs. I drove around one particular council estate with my door windows wound shut, because as soon as I entered the estate, bricks would be lobbed at my van. The traffic department received orders not to go into this estate because their new cars were being damaged; and on a couple of occasions bullets were fired at the police vans.

Just inside the estate was a petrol station; the national press had named it the most dangerous petrol station in Britain, and because it was situated on the main route through the city and on the edge of the estate, many workers on their way home from Manchester pulled into this petrol station. The majority of these workers hadn't a clue about personal safety, leaving their doors unlocked and leaving their personal property on display inside their vehicles. Mobile phones had just been introduced into society and were a fantastic prize for any thief. As soon as the drivers went to pay inside the station, the dark shadows of the thieves crept out of the estate and walked straight up to the unlocked vehicles to help themselves with whatever they wanted. This happened five or six times a night, and by the time the police attended through the rush hour traffic; the thieves were at home admiring their loot. With their hoods up and scarves over their faces the thieves even walked between the lines of queuing traffic, to see if there was anything inside the occupied cars they fancied stealing. Motorists who had never encountered this breed of human being before had the shock of their lives. I felt sorry for them because they tasted my world for a few minutes, and some single females would scream hysterically, refusing to open their car door, even to the police! Drivers visiting the petrol station, sometimes returned to their vehicles and came face to face with these street urchins. Because they had never encountered a thief in their lifetime, they froze. The odd motorists, including a barrister, tried to retrieve their property, but after a few minutes of struggling they were out of breath and surrendered to the thieves. The majority of the car thieves were aged between 13 and 18 years-old and were extremely violent.

Our supervision didn't have a clue what to do; they were too busy wondering how to stop all the armed robberies and car thefts to even care about a few kids nicking from cars. A new townie Inspector who hadn't worked in a city before became in charge of our shift. One day before our tour of duty started, the matter of the petrol station thefts was mentioned. I devised a plan to catch the thieves, but our Inspector said we didn't have the resources to carry out the plan and to everybody's amazement, suggested: 'Has anybody tried talking to these children?'

The constables glanced toward each other, then seemed to think 'Get back in your office and shut the fuck up.'

As we didn't have the resources, I parked on the station forecourt every spare minute I had. It appeared to be having a positive effect; however, one evening I parked my van on the forecourt and a split second after applying my handbrake, I heard a loud bang; followed by an excruciating pain in my left arm. I looked to my left and noticed the passenger door window smashed and a large brick on the floor near to my feet. My first thought was, 'What a fucking shot.'

I looked into the darkness for the culprit, but whoever had bricked me had long gone. With no chance of finding them I shouted up over the radio informing the communications room, which left me feeling how the public felt when it took twenty minutes for another police van to attend through the busy traffic. Again, it wasn't reported in the injury on duty book, as it was just a cut and a large bruise.

The bosses reported it to the local newspaper and the headlines that day read, 'Danger kids gang attack police.' The write up explained how a policeman was injured after his van was stoned on the forecourt of Britain's most dangerous petrol station, it also explained that more than 200 attacks had been carried out on motorists and their cars by a gang of untouchable child criminals. At the end of the report on the damage to my vehicle, it also mentioned a police van had been hot-wired and stolen nearby; which wasn't unusual if you left your police van unattended.

On one occasion, two officers on my shift attended a domestic incident in one of the tower blocks and as there were no other patrols available, they left their van unattended. Upon returning to their van they discovered the windows had been smashed and their helmets had been stolen. The officers reported this to their supervision who disciplined them for leaving their helmets in the van, not the kind of support an officer needs.

After the attack on my vehicle the station bosses created a video unit, most of the officers who staffed this unit were overweight bobbies who had been sat in offices throughout most of their career. They were not much use on the street, so they got sent on a course to gather evidence by videoing offences, the video recorders were the size of small suitcases and VHS videotapes were used to record any action. The unit managed to get permission to film from a business premises opposite the petrol station and over a period of six months; they recorded and gathered evidence on several teenage criminals who had been stealing from cars. On lad who was only 13 years-old was filmed trying to get into a vehicle which was locked and inside this vehicle sat a single female driver. Frustrated because the vehicle was locked, he threw a car spark plug into the passenger door window, causing it to smash. Amazingly, the spark plug flew past the face of the female and smashed her driver's door window, the criminal then calmly reached into the car and took a mobile phone. Because the video unit wanted to keep their observation point a secret, it was months before the kid was arrested. He went to court and because of his age, was bailed to go home and return to court at a later date. The day he was released on bail from court he committed two more thefts, which was why these children were deemed untouchable. A few years later he was arrested after committing armed robberies at post offices—the usual step-up for these kids.

I continued to play the figures game and would take pleasure in stopping criminals' cars, which few officers had the bottle to do on their own. Because they had got used to being stopped by me they slipped up with the occasional snippet of intelligence. The city's criminals were well known for not being grasses and would never want to be seen talking to the police, it gave me great satisfaction when they opened up. Knowing how devious they could be, I knew the information they let 'slip' could be malicious. I would never give them any personal information about myself, especially about being married with children. The criminals I stopped were not to be trusted for one second, but we needed to tolerate each other—up to a point.

Police supervisors had been under pressure to get off their arses and spend more time on the streets, unfortunately our new Inspector chose to go out with me during an afternoon shift. I thought of lots of excuses not to take him out but none of my excuses worked, so I reluctantly took him out and headed straight for the petrol station estate. Not long after driving onto the estate, I spotted a car full of criminals who featured on Fred's gang chart; I flashed my lights, signalling the driver to pull the car over. All four got out and immediately started the game of abuse and under-handed threats. This was just banter and I knew they were just trying it on; but the Inspector panicked, shouting over his radio for back-up; he had been used to outer town policing and the criminals doing what they were told. I continued talking to the criminals, faced the abuse, and ended up having a laugh with them. The Inspector had backed off to my van and didn't hear what was being said; his efforts were spent on rushing the back-up van to the area to assist. Finally, to the Inspector's relief the van turned up, but I waved them on saying they weren't required. I handed the driver a producer for my tick in the book and he drove away with his mates. The Inspector and

I got back into our van and I could see he had lost his bottle.

He tried to turn it on me saying 'You should never talk and laugh with those type of people,' at which point I reminded him of his comments about talking to the children. The Inspector didn't ask to be taken out again—he never left the station.

Being a policeman seemed to be my dominant identity, and I put lots of thought into this role. I also put a lot of effort into my identity as a loving father and husband. I still lived in my two-up two-down terraced house, but instead of going home and relaxing I still had to be vigilant. My car had been stolen on three occasions from the front of my house and burglars had cleared out my house a few times. Once, when my mini metro was stolen, I phoned the police telling them it wouldn't have gone far because there was only two pounds of petrol in it. After a few minutes they phoned me back saying it had been abandoned on the M62 motorway, in the middle of nowhere. When I went to pick it up, I noticed the thieves had ripped the ignition coving and it had been hot-wired. I laughed out loud because the thieves would have had to walk miles to get to civilisation; I knew there was a reason I only put two quid in it. Not being able to afford to repair it, I spent months hot-wiring my car each morning to get it started.

On one occasion I was burgled when I was at work and the burglars battered my dog with a stick; we didn't have much to take apart from the vacuum cleaner and video recorder. My neighbour the ex-cop was also burgled, and they left some dry-cleaning tokens on his backdoor step, which had the name of the force he was in, which was obviously a piss take by the burglars. Then one hot summer's night after I had finished work, I sat in my living room watching TV when my attention was drawn to a teenage lad walking along my street; I noticed he was wearing a thick bob hat and woolly gloves. Now, I'm no Inspector Morse, but even I knew there was something dodgy about him. I watched him walk down the street and behind the row of terraced houses opposite my house. I gave him a few minutes before going to investigate. As I peeped over the back wall of one of the terraced houses, I saw the same lad trying to prize open the ground floor window with a screwdriver; I sneaked up behind him and tackled him to the floor. After the initial shock, he tried to stab me with the screwdriver, I pinned his head down with my knee and took the screwdriver from his grip. Another neighbour phoned the police who arrived 20 minutes later; twenty minutes kneeling on somebody's head takes some doing and us not having have much to talk about, made it seem longer.

A scruffy overweight bobby approached me and asked what I had seen; after I told him what I had witnessed, he lethargically turned to his colleague saying, 'What shall we do with him?'

I hadn't told the officers I was in the police force so I turned around and advised them, 'how about arrest him for attempted burglary for a start?'

Reluctantly they took him off my hands, and I wrote my own evidence statement saving them time. I never booked myself back on duty and was on a knife edge for the next few weeks in case he came back to get revenge. This lad was part of a team of burglars from a neighbouring town and was sentenced to five years' imprisonment. The cops who took him away never contacted me again and the supervision covering the area where I lived never contacted me either. A well-done would have sufficed, but no; nothing at all, I had caught a burglar red-handed, spent most of the night writing a statement and put the safety of my own property and family in jeopardy.

'No wonder nobody else gives a fuck,' I thought. However, I felt good for my elderly neighbours who lived in the street for years who could now feel safer. There wasn't another burglary in my street for another 6 months so the team of burglars must have gone elsewhere. Meanwhile, back at work, the amount of theft from cars had increased, and nobody seemed to do anything about the situation.

To give us a better chance of catching the thieves, I came up with a plan to get a few old mountain bikes and ride around in our own clothes. I went over my Inspector's head and put my ideas through the Detective Inspector, who said it would be a great idea. He then authorised four of my shift to work 2 hours overtime each night. It was great, wearing our own clothing and feeling like a normal person again, and still being paid a wage. I think the reason this tactic hadn't been used before was because the police stood out so much; the majority were 6-foot-tall with side partings and a moustache; they were also stiff and ridged. Times had changed and some cops including myself didn't fit the stereotypical image of a policeman and found it easier to blend in with the public. My first confidence boost was when I cycled around one of the high crime areas and parked my bike up for a rest. As I did I saw a large figure walking down the street towards me, who I recognised as being a male high up in the rank structure of the gang and a person who had appeared on national TV, threatening to shoot his own son because he was an informant. As he approached, I felt he knew I was a police officer and I may as well have been wearing my police helmet. I tried not to pay much attention to him and was shocked when he spoke.

'All right, lad, be careful, there's two cop cars in the next street.'

Stunned, I just said 'cheers.'

I mumbled the reply, as I didn't have a Manchester accent and didn't want to raise suspicion. As he walked away after doing his good deed for the day I relaxed, having passed an important test. About an hour later I spotted a lad about 14 years-old, walking along the main road looking into parked cars. I shouted up over the radio for my colleagues to cover the opposite end of the street. As I crept up on the lad, he picked up a brick and threw it straight through the passenger door window of a parked car; I was only five feet away from him and he hadn't noticed a thing. He leant into the car helping himself to a mobile phone on the front seat; as he removed himself from the car I grabbed him. This was fantastic as I couldn't get better evidence, and along with this crime, he admitted to several others. The Detective Inspector cracked open a bottle of whiskey because we had detected a few crimes for him; but our own Inspector tried to put a downer on things by saying we shouldn't be cycling around the streets with no lights on our bikes! I tried to point out to him that no criminal I knew had lights on their bikes, and we may as well have blue flashing lights on the bikes. This didn't impress the ex-traffic officer, or a 'traffic-wank' as they were commonly known, and he threatened to discipline me if I didn't display lights.

I came across this a few times during the time I spent in the police, when a supervisors' pride and stubbiness makes you think 'oh fuck off, I won't do it then.' These thoughts didn't last long because I wanted to catch the bad guys.

Luckily, I didn't have to work for this Inspector anymore, as an eight-month attachment had been advertised to join the station's proactive unit. This unit dealt with lots of crime-related incidents and the officers always wore their own clothes. The Detective Inspector interviewed me for this place and I had no problem getting the job. In 1996, I walked into the proactive unit in my civilian clothes and realised this was what I wanted to be doing. There were plenty of experienced police officers handpicked for the role in this office.

Class A drugs hit the North West of England, but not in this particular city. The gang leaders deemed drugs like heroin and crack cocaine to be dirty drugs and the gang was so tight, they would not tolerate heroin addicts, because these weak people became snitches and informants. But the money to be made by selling these so-called dirty drugs was too tempting and a within the next few years a new breed of criminals brought them into the city, with devastating effect.

The officers within the proactive unit had only been dealing with the Class B drugs cannabis and amphetamine, this being their only knowledge about illegal drugs. I had an inkling a change would soon happen, and dirty drugs would be introduced into the city, I was ready to watch the development with a beady eye. The proactive unit would give me all the tools I required to be ready for the wave of violence which flowed towards the city. The majority of the unit were older officers who liked to stay in the station, although some younger officers liked to play out. I kept hold of the mountain bikes which I'd appropriated in uniform and hit the streets—without lights!

I rode into the petrol station estate where my van had been bricked and immediately got results, catching thieves breaking into vehicles. If they weren't caught stealing from vehicles, they normally carried a tool on them for breaking into vehicles or possessed cannabis, so arresting them was easy. The sneakier I was the better, and I spent as much of my shift out of the station and on the streets; the criminals wondered when I was going to pop up. Not only could I use the mountain bikes, I could now use unmarked police vehicles, observation vans and I also went on an optical evidence gathering course which showed me how to use the video recorders. I spent hours videoing offenders, but it was much better to mix things up by also being on the streets. Some older officers would spend too much time videoing and not enough time getting stuck into and knowing who the criminals were.

Like any other proactive unit, we became involved in drugs warrants at peoples' addresses and seized lots of cannabis and amphetamines. On one occasion when I was in charge of the search, we seized two TV satellite decoders and arrested the male at the address. I arrested this male on suspicion of theft, then took him to the police station. He gave a few false names, which wasn't unusual, but we eventually worked out his true identity. I couldn't identify the decoders from their serial numbers so I planned on interviewing then releasing him so I could make further enquiries for when he returned. His solicitor arrived at the police station and I took them both down to the interview room to have a consultation. After five minutes, the solicitor walked towards me to ask a question. I was furious with him as he shouldn't have left my prisoner unattended. Upon returning to the interview room I saw it was empty; I looked up, and twenty feet above my head I saw a smashed skylight.

'Oh fuck' I thought and shouted for assistance to search for the escapee. My prisoner had escaped; he had climbed out of the building and disappeared into thin air. After searching for about thirty minutes I gave up—he had gone. I informed the solicitor that his client had escaped and he tried his best to look shocked. I wondered to myself why he had escaped from a police station just because of a few decoders. The most he would have been facing was a handling charge.

I loved going home, my children were young and waited at the front door with outstretched arms, shouting 'daddy, daddy!' My heart melted because of the love filling our family home. I hadn't been listening to music, unusual for me; but I watched Disney films over and over again whilst sat alongside my children. The city I worked in was a strange place, the youngsters didn't appear to have an interest in anything apart from getting pissed, fighting or committing crime. The ones I had dealings with didn't listen to music, watch or play sport. Could I have been morphing into their mentality?

It always made me laugh when I saw the public outside Manchester following bands like the Happy Mondays, Oasis and Ian Brown who were being 'mad for it.' I used to think to myself, 'meet one of these Mancunians' who you admire and try so hard to imitate, and you could forget about music. This would be far too creative and consist of a legal form of enjoyment. And when you are trying to copy their Manchester accent to fit in; they will rip your fucking throats out.

Ecstasy was a big money-maker in the cities during this time, but the criminals didn't go to the clubs to enjoy the atmosphere, they just wanted to make money and intimidate people. Admitting to having a fondness for music would have been regarded as a sign of weakness amongst the criminals.

A week after my prisoner escaped I was relaxing at home reading the local free paper and saw an article showing a shopkeeper holding a machete. The articles headline read: 'Kung foo shopkeeper fights off armed raiders.' It described how four armed raiders, wearing balaclavas and armed with sticks and machetes, entered an electrical shop, threatened the shopkeeper and stole some electrical items. The raiders had intended to steal more, but the shopkeeper who was trained in the martial arts fought back, and the raiders ran away with not much gain.

'Good lad' I thought, and I laughed as I imagined these bullies getting a taste of their own medicine. After reading more I became very interested after seeing two TV satellite digital decoders had been stolen during the robbery.

'Surely not?' I thought. This was about fifteen miles away from where I seized the stolen decoders. My curiosity got the better of me and I asked my wife to pass me the phone. I rang the electrical shop and spoke directly to the 'kung foo hero'. I asked him to describe the stolen property, and the description matched perfectly, so I arranged to phone him the following day to check the serial numbers. I phoned him as arranged and he gave me the serial numbers, which to my delight matched the ones I had seized. Bingo! Now I knew why my prisoner had been so keen to escape. I spent all of Christmas hunting down my prisoner and eventually caught him. The shopkeeper identified him in a line-up because luckily he had pulled two of the males' balaclavas off during the struggle. My prisoner was sentenced to five years' imprisonment for his part in the attack and I could relax again.

The relaxation period quickly passed because cars were still being broken into on the petrol station forecourt. Following the brick being thrown through my window, I had a bee in my bonnet about this place; although I had caught a few of them they were still at it. Once I joined the proactive unit, I found myself in a better position to do something about it; I planned an operation which would catch the thieves in the act. The estate where the thieves lived was enclosed by three main roads, which at rush hour were grid locked, and uniformed police took ages to get there so catching the thieves seemed impossible. I got hold of two transit vans with sliding doors and two unmarked cars. My plan involved placing one officer in each of the unmarked cars, then we placed one fake mobile phone on the passenger seat and another on the dashboard of each car. Each car would be closely followed by a transit van, which had four police officers in the rear and two in the front. Officers drove a car and a van through the heavy traffic, followed by the other car and a van who had positioned themselves about a quarter of a mile behind them.

After an hour of driving around the estate, the first van shouted up over closed radio channel; 'four little twats have come out of the estate and are walking through the lines of traffic, looking into cars.' This was our chance and I wasn't going to miss it. I sat in the front seat of the second van and as we approached the petrol station I observed four youths in dark clothing with their hoods up. 'Please go for our mobile phones,' I thought.

As we approached, the thieves walked in-between the traffic and approached a BMW driven by a single female. They looked inside of the BMW and within seconds threw a brick through the passenger window then grabbed a handbag.

'Go, go, go' I shouted, it felt like being in the Bill and at the red phone boxes at the same time. We all jumped out of the vans and within seconds the four lads were shouting out in agony as they were pinned face-first to the concrete. Drivers in the traffic que sounded their horns and cheered, this must have been the first time they were happy to be stuck in traffic. The thieves were charged and given conditions by the court not walk on that road again. Because we had stepped up our tactics to catch them, the thieves became very wary stealing from cars and the incidents almost stopped. Also because of the publicity and pressure from the authorities, the petrol station was demolished.

As I didn't have much cash, my own clothes started to get minging and going out in the rain made my trainers smell terrible. I smelt worse than some of the criminals and a few of them commented they were better off than me. I couldn't argue with these comments, and knew I needed to smarten up after a detective sergeant named me 'Stig of the dump.' Before the name calling got worse, I asked Kath to take me on a shopping spree where she treated me to some new training shoes and a pair of £25 jeans. The comment from Kath was, 'you'd better make them last.' I turned up at the station and had the piss taken out of my bright white trainers, I felt like a child who had been bought new trainers for their holidays. I didn't want to brag off about my new clothes, so I went straight out on patrol.

As I drove around the streets with another colleague, we spotted a male; the first ever prisoner who had escaped from Group 4 security. Group four took over the prison escorts from the police, so it would be a feather in our cap to catch him. I slowly drove up to him but as he was on high alert, he spotted my vehicle and started to run. I jumped out of my car and chased him on foot. He approached the side of a pub and I thought he had nowhere to go, I could see the headlines. To my surprise, he scrambled up a fifteen-foot fence and jumped over it. Even though I wasn't great with heights I was determined he wasn't getting away, so I scrambled over the fence and once I reached the top, jumped; as I did my jeans got caught in barbed wire and ripped as I fell to the floor.

I continued to chase the male but kept thinking 'my fucking new jeans, she's gonna kill me.'

I caught the male and went back to the station. The back of my leg was dripping in blood, which pumped out of two gaping holes. I wasn't bothered about the holes in my leg; telling Kath about the damage to my £25 jeans worried me more. After pleading with her for a couple of weeks Kath bought me a new pair of jeans for £10, and I never bought expensive jeans again. I didn't need to worry though, because my 8-month attachment was over. I returned to uniformed duties and could wear the clothes provided by my police force. I spent a short time patrolling the streets as a section officer but soon had the chance to apply for the drugs unit.

Chapter five

No matter what

I spent the last few months on uniformed patrol playing the performance indicator game. This involved stopping people I had come into contact with whilst I was on the proactive unit. I kept in contact with a few criminals who gave me information, these people were known as informants, snouts, snitches or grasses. The city's criminals hated grasses and saw them as the lowest of the low, but most criminals didn't want to go to jail and would do almost anything to prevent this happening, which included giving information regarding the criminal activities others were committing. I realised the lower ranking criminals were proud not to branded as grasses and were less likely to inform than the criminals higher up the structure. This was 1997 and very hard to keep in contact with informants; it's hard to believe life without mobile phones, but they hadn't been fully introduced to the public and the main way of keeping in touch would be by stopping them on the street or calling at their home address. Both ways were fraught with danger and I had to be extremely careful, because I wanted none of the people talking seriously injured or murdered.

It worked both ways though, the criminals weren't stupid and because of their need to protect themselves, they were always attempting to get a police officer on their books. It didn't matter how long you had been in the police or how high up you were in the police ranks, if an officer wasn't careful the criminals would have the officer in the palm of their hand. I always thought a solid line between the criminals and the police existed, but over the years I saw a number of officers and criminals cross this line; once crossed, unless they landed very lucky or didn't give a toss, they would find themselves walking about inside a mountain of shit. In the seventies and eighties officers dealt with informants with the mind set 'you scratch my back and Ill scratch yours,' and the officers would be rewarded by the criminals.

When I dealt with informants, it would be 'I'll scratch your back and give you a couple of hundred quid for the two minutes of information you have provided, and I'll deal with the mountains of paperwork after I've arrested someone.' I used to think to myself 'who's the mug? Him with his constant supply of money or me, broke, driving around in a battered old mini metro and wearing stinky training shoes?' It made little sense, but it had to be done because I wanted to catch the criminals in this game of cat and mouse.

After being interviewed they gave me a date to start in the drugs unit. I always wanted to join the drugs unit after I saw the drugs and licensing unit when I first joined the police. It was a small unit who visited public houses to check if the landlord served alcohol after time; they also investigated Jamaican shebeens, where people smoked cannabis, and alcohol was sold without a licence. Although there weren't many Jamaicans living in the area I worked, stolen property and cannabis were sold in the pubs; unless it was owned by the Quality Street gang where nothing happened because they were places where the senior detectives drank after work. The officers working in the drugs and licensing unit had long hair and wore their own clothes, but times were changing and the introduction of Class A drugs meant that they would soon be out of touch.

The licensing part of the unit was dropped, as drugs were becoming a major problem, so it became the drugs unit. Heroin and crack had been introduced to Moss Side in the late eighties/early nineties and everything had started to bubble on the streets with daily shootings—glamorous to outsiders but a frightening place to live. This new wave of drug dealing and violence took the police force by surprise. The supply of heroin and crack cocaine brought in bundles of money, and addicts queued up for the small packages of powder. Their lives were being ripped apart, and so desperate for their next hit, they became easy targets for the police to turn into informants. The criminals operating in the city I worked in didn't want this situation, so the leaders of the gang made every effort to keep these hard drugs out. They made lots of money from cleaner drugs such as ecstasy, amphetamine and cannabis, along with money made from their other criminal activities. So they didn't want these dirty drugs ruining their well-organised set-up by encouraging a city full of police informants. Unfortunately for them, this new drug scene would not be defeated and conquered everything that went before it, ripping the gang apart. I found myself bang in the middle of this explosion.

Home life was great, my children were growing up, my wife got a job at a bank near to where I worked. We bought another car for £100 so Kath could drive to work, and I started my new job in the drugs unit. With the extra income, I could smarten up my appearance and would not be called 'Stig of the dump' again.

On the first day in the drugs unit Coolios' song 'Gangster's paradise' played on my car radio on the way to work. Could this be a sign of things to come? I hoped not. Not enjoying this song, I placed my Angelic Upstarts tape in the radio cassette: 'who killed Liddle? Did you kill Liddle? Who killed Liddle? Police killed Liddle Towers' blasted out of my radio and took me back to my youth club days. Halfway through 'The murder of Liddle Towers,' the tape got chewed up inside the cassette. 'Just turn the fucking thing off,' I thought, which I did, then drove to work in silence wondering what the drugs unit had in store for me.

I entered the drugs unit office with enthusiasm, looking forward to the challenges ahead of me and having a sneaky feeling in the back of my head that interesting times may be just around the corner.

My first mission was to meet the rest of the drugs unit. The unit had been restructured, and the Sergeant pointed out a weedy lad sat in the corner.

'That's the rest of the drugs unit, you and him will be the drugs unit and the proactive unit will support you whenever you need them.' The drugs unit space in the office comprised of one table; I sat opposite the weedy lad and to my surprise he was a cockney, but everybody to the south of Wigan was a cockney in my eyes. Cockney J, as I called him, was a small and skinny lad who always had a cigarette hanging from his lips and proudly held the title of being the most assaulted man in the police force. After knowing him, I realised the way he spoke to criminals was why he kept being thumped.

The proactive unit displayed their feelings towards Cockney J and disregarded everything he said. I never joined this group mentality, so I stuck with J and we worked well together. The officers in the proactive unit couldn't understand why I didn't want to join in with their 'anti-J' campaign, which made things uncomfortable for myself and Cockney J. This separated the office, but I wanted to make this drugs unit the best it could be, even if it was just myself and Cockney J.

One or two of the proactive unit had been officers in the old drugs and licensing unit and wanted to prove they were the bee's knees when it came to the drugs side of crime. However, my informants told me something frightening was coming to the city and I felt ready for the task ahead.

I passed this intelligence onto the proactive unit, but with their cock-sure attitudes, they dismissed the seriousness of it. I completed the intelligence reports by filling in an A4 paper form and sent them to the Detective Inspector, who more than likely filed the reports in his office bin.

He wouldn't be able to do this for long, because the information age had kicked in and huge computers found their way into our office. At the beginning they were used to leave messages for each other on what they called an officer's 'scratch pad.' The start of things to come! Officers left a message on your scratch pad to cover their backs, proving they had asked you to do something. To be up to speed with modern technology, I signed a three-year contract and bought a pager so my informants found it easier and safer to keep in touch by sending a message. Shortly after signing into this contract, mobile phones exploded onto the scene and I no longer needed a pager. Could I end the contract though? Could I bollocks.

In the early stages of my time in the drugs unit, we searched addresses and arrested people for the usual offences of possessing cannabis and amphetamine with intent to supply. But one day, in March 1998 everything changed, when myself and Cockney J stopped a car being driven by a skinny white lad, wearing John Lennon-style tinted glasses. Upon searching him we found several wraps of heroin and a mobile phone, which didn't stop ringing—'Fuck me, here it comes,' I thought. The lad was a heroin addict from out of town and to be fair he didn't grass, but possessed a list containing names of local heroin addicts, who I knew travelled out of the city to buy heroin. Heroin was always going to hit the streets, but I couldn't understand how this skinny lad was able to deal it in this area, when it had been kept out so long—surely the main gang leader, who I named the Prime Minister, wouldn't let this happen in 'his' city? If he was aware this lad was dealing in the city, he would have stopped it. Or would he? Maybe he didn't know, I didn't mind because this was why I had joined the drug unit. I had been waiting eagerly for it to happen.

Around the time we stopped John Lennon, two lads riding a motorbike and brandishing a machine gun fired shots at the Prime minister who was standing with a few of his friends. The lads missed their intended target and the bullets ended up embedded in the gable end of a council house on the petrol station estate. Following the shooting, the two lads laid low at a caravan park in Wales but fell out with the locals and fired their machine gun at them. They fled Wales after this incident, but one was arrested in possession of the machine gun whilst he waited for a train, and the other who I knew as the 'Little fella' returned to the city to play a prominent part in a drugs war.

Intelligence suggested that the Prime Minister had been shot at because of an argument over drugs; the general opinion was the two lads responsible might not live long, but weeks passed and nothing happened to them. Word on the street was the PM hadn't been as 'hands-on' as he once was, and this new breed of criminals, 'the young firm,' intended to introduce heroin to the city no matter what the consequences were. The young firm spread fear across the whole of Manchester and other criminals waited, nervously.

I stopped the local criminals to find out what was happening, and as a sign of their appreciation they sprayed I was a sex case on the side of a terraced house. I didn't have many dealings with the PM, but I knew he had lots of influence on the city's criminals and was well respected by the public; every criminal I stopped claimed to be his relation. He held celebrity status in the city and even the police bosses spoke about him as though he was a film star. He still lived in a council house in what I called the tower-block area. One night on uniformed patrol, I parked up near his house; it wasn't long before he came out of his house, took photographs of me and told me to fuck off. I returned the following night and after being parked up for about ten minutes, two dark shadows came out of an alleyway and threw petrol bombs towards my van. I thought to myself, 'Ok I get your point, not someone to mess around with.'

The PM didn't mess about and had lots of runners to do his dirty work; he was associated with a security firm, but after a while they ran out of work because the offices and pubs they protected burned to the ground after refusing to pay protection money. Visitors to the pubs comprised of the doormen and criminals who had threatened the landlords. Because the landlord wasn't making money, the pubs shut down—that's if the criminals hadn't set fire to them first. Not a well thought-out marketing plan.

In July 1998, the PM proved he was still 'hands-on' by stabbing a man who almost died; after this incident he fled the country. He had been making a film about himself at the time of the incident, but the film crew taped over the stabbing incident with footage of a coke can. Considering the pressure—who blamed them? Part of me felt sorry for the film crew, but another part of me thought they got what they deserved for glamorising crime. The PM had made a mistake; maybe he needed a long break anyway. As the incident happened in part of the city which I didn't cover, I didn't have much to do with the case; my only involvement was to search the living quarters of the pub where the film crew had been staying and I could only imagine the panic after the incident. This incident didn't interest me, as something else occupied my mind: 'what happens now?' It wasn't long before I found the answer.

It may have been a coincidence, but as soon as the PM went on the run, everything unfolded. I spent hours in observation posts monitoring and trying to work out this unfolding. On one occasion, I observed a known location from the eighth floor of a tower-block flat, and it was impossible to see me from the ground. To my surprise, known criminals came out of their house on the street below and waved at me. I couldn't figure out how they knew I was in this flat, so high up from the ground. The flat I used was an empty property owned by the council, and it transpired that the criminals had a council worker in their pocket who informed them I had entered the flat. I wondered, 'who are these people, the fucking mafia?'

Another occasion I had to enter the second floor flat of a maisonette block, right in the centre of the tower-block area. The flat I entered was the only empty flat in the building, I needed a good disguise or else I would be recognised. I found the scruffiest clothes I could, and wore a pair of jam jar bottomed spectacles and as the VHS video recorder was so large, I needed to carry it in a large holdall. I entered the flat very early in the morning with my hood up, pretending to limp and dragging the holdall behind me; if someone saw me, they would have thought I was nuts. Because the proactive were busy with another job and Cockney J was off work, I had to enter alone. As soon as I gained entry to the flat, I felt relieved that my first mission was over; I needed to get out at some point, but with luck, I would have collected some evidence of drug dealing on video. After about an hour my neighbours in the flat above woke up, and I could hear them moving around their flat. Then the worst thing possible happened—my new neighbours started to play Boyzone's 'No matter what,' on full volume, then replayed it and replayed it for six hours—non-fucking stop!

There wasn't much movement on the streets and I was beginning to get a headache when after a few hours I heard somebody knocking on my flat door. I tip-toed up to the door and peeped through the peephole. My heart stopped; I saw a large white man with a goatee beard and ponytail stood in front of my door, looking towards the peephole. In his right hand, he held a long kitchen knife down by his side—just like a serial-fucking-killer. I tried not to breathe, move or even blink because I was sure this killer would have noticed any of these actions. To my relief, after a few minutes he turned and walked away. In my head, I knew he was looking for me; but somehow I convinced myself he wanted to kill the 'Boyzone fucker' above me. To be sure, I sat still for half-an-hour; during this time, I watched a bluebottle flying up and down the window I had been filming from, attempting to free himself from the flat; I knew how he felt. With nothing to do, the punk song 'I am the fly' sung by 'Wire' played inside my head. When I was sure the serial killer had left, I began to film again.

I didn't have to wait long before I saw two males who I knew to be heroin addicts, waiting in an enclosed car park just beneath my position. I watched them lingering for about twenty minutes, then noticed a Ford Ka occupied by two lads drive into the enclosed car park. To my utter enjoyment, a deal took place right in front of me which I captured on film. The car, a hire car, was hired out to a lad who lived out of town. I knew from this moment that the city's heroin gang, the 'young firm', were using these outer towners to deal their heroin. I returned to show my Sergeant the evidence and attempted to convince him we had enough to strike on the vehicle. The Sergeant was pleased with the development, but the proactive had their own operation in progress, which involved undercover officers being deployed on the streets to try and purchase heroin.

Even though the proactive unit hadn't bothered to inform the drug unit they planned this drugs operation, I felt pleased they were combatting the heroin trade. My only knowledge of undercover operations were ones which took place in Moss Side during the early nineties. I had concerns though; Moss Side had developed as a drug dealing market, the city I worked in hadn't, which made it more dangerous for the undercover officers. Whilst the proactive unit were making plans to put their undercover operation into place, I continued to drive around the tower-block area attempting to put everything into place. One day I was out driving near to where I filmed the drug deals taking place in the car park, when several lads leaving a public house gripped my attention. I observed them and couldn't believe what I saw; this group was the most intimidating sight I had ever seen. On their own they frightened the shit out of people, but to see them together made me stop in my tracks and think—'Shit, this isn't good.'

I couldn't put a name to everyone; I did see the Big fella, the Little fella, Mr Bates, the Knife, Rupert the Bear, Mr Clever and the Red Indian, the rest looked just as intimidating. There was a reason why this meeting had taken place and it wasn't flower arranging.

The group split up, and I stopped Rupert the Bear who just said, 'fuck me, Officer, you're buzzing.'

He was right; I was buzzing and my heart was pumping out of my chest, because I knew this meeting would produce something big, horrible, and downright nasty. I reported the sighting to my supervision, who didn't have the time to understand the developments, they were too busy with the proactive operation. The higher bosses in the station couldn't get any help, as many of the specialist squads wouldn't work in this city because it had too many bent cops, and it wasn't safe for them. The criminals I observed leaving the pub were too small for the national squads and below their radar. This meant that it was myself and Cockney J who had the responsibility of monitoring this menace.

The Big fella led the gang; he had been in prison for kidnapping drug dealers and torturing them; a feared man in the criminal world and related to the PM, this may have explained why the lads who shot at the PM had not been murdered; because they 'grafted' for the Big fella. The first time I came into contact with him was when I stopped his vehicle, just after he'd been released from prison following his kidnapping sentence.

The Big fella just stared straight through me, saying, 'just do what you have to, Officer, and let me go on my way.' No anger or frustration in his voice—just cold and chilling.

The Little fella easily took the prize for the most violent, dangerous criminal I ever came into contact with. He possessed a string of convictions for violence—an armed robber who wouldn't think twice about shooting the security guards. I first met him in the police cells. The prisons were overflowing and the police minded the prisoners for the prisons. He assaulted almost every police officer he came into contact with, and forever punched the walls and did press-ups; he constantly spoke about kidnapping and torturing a police officer.

The Red Indian—a man mountain of muscle, extremely violent who's favourite weapon was a machete. I first came into contact with this male when I saw him in a public park; crossed-legged and wearing a Red Indian head-dress. A warrant had been issued by the courts for his arrest, I got him into my van by speaking to him like a parent would to their child, he was spaced out on this occasion; thank God.

Rupert the Bear—the only criminal I could have a laugh with. I first came into contact with him on the petrol station estate, after he stole from cars or mugged people. Once I searched his bedroom after arresting him, and discovered all his Rupert the Bear annuals hidden under his bed. He begged me not to tell anybody about them; I didn't, but hummed the 'Rupert the Bear' theme tune each time I stopped him with his gangster mates—he didn't give me any lip.

Mr Clever—previous convictions for violence; used heroin himself and a link to the outer towns when the young firm began supplying heroin. Mr Clever confirmed to me what nobody else wanted to hear: 'they kept it out, we are bringing it in' was his comment after arrest.

The Knife—didn't last too long with the group, as he found himself on a murder charge after stabbing another male to death on the petrol station estate. This wasn't connected to the drug scene, but just showed the level of violence these males used. When a female detective interviewed him for the murder, he played footsie under the table, and winked at her.

Mr Bates—another violent robber; the police received many reports from members of the public, whose car windows had been smashed by Mr Bates. If he suspected the police were following him, he would stop, and attack the car with a baseball bat. He got it wrong every time, and there were a lot of very shocked and terrified civilians with smashed window screens.

MACHETE GANG
HACK OFF ARM

A few days after my sighting of the meeting, the heroin gang became every drug dealers' worst nightmare. I responded to a few incidents in the tower-block area where people had been chopped up by a male brandishing a machete. The assaulted lads were drug dealers, and off the record they said the Red Indian attacked them. One night whilst sat at home with my children, I heard an explosion. It wasn't long before I found out a shotgun had been used to blast the front door of a terraced house two streets from where I lived; the occupants had been viciously attacked with machetes.

I instantly recognised from the method of the attack that the young firm were responsible. They then assaulted another male inside his home, five minutes' walk from my home. These addresses were 12 miles from the tower-block area. A few days later a lad was attacked in his home two miles from where I lived. The offenders used machetes and almost killed the male who ended up having his hand amputated;

the Red Indian was later arrested for this attack. The heroin gang put pressure on the established drug territories in neighbouring towns, and unfortunately for me one of these towns was where I lived. Reports came in that dealers had been being stabbed up their arse, shot and lost their hands during the machete attacks. Lots of these incidents went unreported, because grassing would bring more trouble to their doorsteps.

At the beginning of the wave of violence, I went to search a drug dealer's address in the tower-block area. The door proved hard to force open and before we gained entry, the occupant threw himself out of his own first-floor bedroom window. I ran downstairs to speak to the male who had clearly broken his leg and displayed cuts to his face caused from the jump. I identified myself as a police officer and he said, 'fuck me, if I knew it was you lot, I would have opened the door.'

This male thought the young firm had come for him; under his settee he stashed a loaded revolver, ready to use, but his fear was so intense he felt a loaded gun didn't offer him enough protection. Because the violent incidents which were being reported occurred on neighbouring areas, it was the responsibility of that area's supervision to investigate. Therefore, even though my supervision had an idea our criminals committed the offences, the crimes didn't affect them, as they hadn't happened on 'their' patch.

From my observations, I saw the Ford Ka which I had filmed still knocking around the streets and I was desperate to strike on it, but the undercover operation was soon to start and hopefully the officers would buy heroin from the occupants of the Ford Ka. The plan was to deploy undercovers within the tower-block area, pretending to be university students with heroin addictions. I wasn't too comfortable with this plan, because the officers appeared to be too clean, and the heroin market in this area was tight. All the addicts knew one another, so it would be difficult to gain trust from them. I wasn't running the operation, so I had no say in the matter.

After about two weeks the officers obtained a telephone number for a heroin dealer, they phoned the number hoping to order heroin and an angry male answered shouting, 'We know you're fucking cops, if you don't fuck off we will kidnap you and fuck you up your arses.'

The threats were real and the operation was aborted. It proved to be a hard operation for the officers. Some you win, some you don't, at least they had the nerve to put themselves forward for this almost impossible task.

Although the undercover operation wasn't successful, it meant the proactive officers were released to help me with my enquiries. The gang had taken over the heroin market in the neighbouring towns and started dealing in their own area. This meant they had to get kilos of the stuff—which proved a problem. Nobody wanted to deal with the young firm because they were so violent; and rightly so. It was rumoured that some members of the young firm travelled to Liverpool to try to purchase kilos of heroin; once there, they met up with the Liverpudlians who agreed to sell them heroin. After the meeting, the Scousers left the pub saying they were off to collect the heroin. They didn't return which saved their lives, because the Little fella had two Mac 10 machine guns waiting nearby, and planned to shoot them then steal the heroin. Not having the best of business meetings, they returned to Manchester and purchased a kilo from the Goochy gang. The local dealers who had been attacked with machetes were now ordered to work for the young firm; these local dealers once bought an ounce of heroin for £700, but now had to pay the gang £1,000. The extra three hundred was for protection—even though nobody else would ever dream of threatening them.

At the end of September 1998, two days after the undercover operation had been aborted, I sneaked my way back into the Boyzone flat. I observed and filmed the same vehicle dealing to the same heroin users, at the exact same location. Armed with this further evidence, I convinced my supervision to strike on the vehicle the following day. The strike took place without any issues; the occupants of the vehicle were searched and found to be in possession of large quantities of deal size wraps of heroin and crack cocaine. The two lads arrested were dealers from a neighbouring town and were subjects of the great 'takeover'.

The young firm were not happy with these arrests on their own patch and grew frustrated because they couldn't establish a heroin market in their own city. An informant warned me to wear body armour all the time, because the Little fella had possession of a Mac 10 machine gun and he planned on shooting me. He also planned to execute a dealer from Moss Side, who had the nerve to enter his area to deal heroin. The Moss Side dealer had made an appearance during my observations, then suddenly stopped entering the city; somebody must have warned him. Basically, the Little fella wanted to kill anybody who pissed him off!

This caused me a lot of concern and to my horror, after I submitted an intelligence reports about the threats, nothing was done about them nor were they even spoken about by my superior officers, it was a case of 'just get on with it'. My bosses didn't understand or care what danger officers and the public were in, I'd been threatened lots of times before, but this was different. A lot of the supervision only passed through my station to gain their 'inner city experience,' which they required to climb further up the promotion ladder.

I had no other choice but to get on with it and soon noticed that the tower-block area came alive with heroin dealers. It was important to gain knowledge about every one of them, before the situation became too big to handle; so, my intention was to disrupt them as much as I could, as I was being paid to do this. I arrested a few users for possession of heroin and they all seemed over the moon they now had a local marketplace to buy their heroin. They also made it crystal clear Mr Clever was the middle man between the young firm and the street users. Even though Mr Clever was a serious criminal, he now used heroin and had more in common with the street users.

At the beginning of October, I stopped one dealer from the Ford Ka, driving a red van outside a user's house in the tower-block area. The male had been released on bail whilst his case was waiting to go to court. To my surprise, Mr Clever was also in the van and wanted on warrant; so, I arrested him. They didn't have any drugs on them but it confirmed Mr Clever's involvement in the drug dealing set-up. A week later, I along with the proactive unit, executed a drugs warrant at Mr Clever's brothers' house. I arrested both Mr Clever and his brother for possession of weed with intent to supply. Class B drugs weren't what I wanted to find, but it kept the pressure on. As I entered the house Mr Clever made a comment, saying I had said something about the Little fella. I had said nothing; it puzzled me why he came out with this comment. The heat was on Mr Clever to deal heroin, and maybe he wanted the Little fella to put the same pressure on me by shit stirring.

I charged Mr Clever with the cannabis offence, but he would soon be charged and convicted of a more serious offence. I continued to stop and speak to users in the area and an informant told me that the gang had become very pissed off with me because they couldn't get their drugs market up and running—he warned me to be very careful.

More graffiti appeared about me on the walls in the tower-block area, in thick white paint. One work of art stated that I was a 'WA.' I never found out what they meant because the creator ran out of wall. Maybe it was going to read a WArm and friendly person? I'll never know.

Mr Clever spent a lot more time around the tower-block area, shagging a young female heroin addict. I spent time observing the woman's address, before gaining enough intelligence to obtain a drugs warrant. In November 1998, I along with the proactive unit, forced entry into the address, and upon entering I saw Mr Clever lying on the living room floor and I saw another lad who I called 'the

Bolt,' sat in a chair. I suspected the Bolt of street dealing as I'd seen him knocking around the tower-block area. He had been in prison for almost killing a police officer by stabbing him in the head with a garden fence rail. Both males struggled during the drugs arrest and Mr Clever even attempted to bite an officers' testicles. Once searched, the Bolt was in possession of about £2,000 worth of crack cocaine and Mr Clever had £500, neatly folded up in his back pocket. In a rage Mr Clever shouted, 'you're a cunt, I know where you live and there's a price on your head.'

This outburst corroborated what my informants told me and although the comment stopped me in my tracks, I still had a job to do as Mr Clever's home address needed searching. At his address, another £450 was seized along with about £2,000 worth of cocaine; this tied them both nicely into the conspiracy. When Mr Clever was being booked into the police station he spoke to other officers, telling them I had a price on my head; something he wouldn't want. I approached him about this comment and he stared at me saying; 'they kept it out—we are bringing it in,' referring to heroin and crack cocaine. Mr Clever had an answer phone message from the Big fella on his mobile phone. The Big fella was furious, shouting, 'where the fuck are you?'

There was another message from the Big fellas' girlfriend; asking if he could 'sort her out,' and I wondered to myself if the Big fella knew Mr Clever was dealing Class A drugs to his girlfriend. The Bolt and Mr Clever got released on bail whilst forensic services analysed the drugs, they were both later charged and sentenced to 4 years in prison. The gang were furious to have lost their middle man and another dealer, but something would happen to make this the least of their worries.

The gang put more and more pressure on other criminals and targeted serious criminals in their own area. I'd been given information that the gang cut up their heroin at a hairdressers' shop in the tower-block area. As nobody else was available to check it out with me, I asked Fred the intelligence officer to come out on a recce. We grabbed an unmarked car and sat observing the hairdressers. Three younger members of the gang entered and left the address; things were looking promising. All of a sudden, a black BMW screeched up in front of our stationary vehicle and out jumped the Little fella and Mr Bates. The Little fellas' eyes popped out of his head, and foam pushed its way out of the sides of his mouth, he named myself and Fred, saying we had become a 'fucking problem to him' and he 'knew where we fucking lived.'

Neither myself nor Fred had taken any handcuffs or body armour out with us and the radios we relied upon were turned down and stashed under our seats—not a wise move. The Little fella kept on reaching inside his jacket, which bulged; I expected to meet his Mac 10 machine gun. Mr Bates screamed that he wanted to twat us, then go home and wank over it. They both shouted that we had been talking 'shit to shit'. The penny then dropped about what Mr Clever had said when we entered his brother's house. To keep on the gang leader's good side, the wanker had been shit stirring. I was concerned when the Little fella then screamed about and named a secret police operation, set up to gather intelligence on the gang; it was obvious there was a leak at the police station.

The way the Little fella was behaving; I expected to be shot any second. I wanted Fred to drive off, but he was one stubborn fucker and wouldn't leave before they did; this would be seen as backing down. I couldn't give a toss, I was shitting myself, I admired Fred for his stubbornness, but could only imagine being peppered with bullets from the Little fellas' machine gun. The Little fella and Mr Bates went back to their car shouting 'We'll see you soon' and 'we are going to count our fucking money.' They then got into their BMW, reversed and smashed into our car before screeching off at speed. As we drove back to the station, it hit me how serious this was. They didn't give a shit about damaging a police vehicle, and had previously surrounded an officer in court threatening him and telling him they would take the assault charge. The officers on the street didn't feel supported, especially from their supervision, so why would they put themselves in risky situations, then face giving evidence in court for a trivial offence. I had given evidence alone against serious criminals, who brought their family and friends along to threaten and abuse me. It's a lonely place. Fred appeared shaken, and this was an officer who had stood on his own facing the Prime Minister and thirty of his followers during a riot. We both had enough experience to know this would be the start of something very dangerous and needed to be on high alert.

A couple of days later, I had finished my shift and drove my car out of the police station; when a dark coloured VW Golf pulled up alongside my vehicle. The hooded front seat passenger looked and pointed a handgun at me before driving off at speed. This was the first day I added an extra 5 miles on my journey home. I had always tried to be aware of vehicles following me, but I now stepped the hyper-vigilance up a few notches. For the next 2-3 years, I used every anti-surveillance moves on my way home, to make sure nobody was following me. I couldn't forgive myself if I led criminals to my front door and put my family at risk. I drove around roundabouts several times, slowed down, sped up, turned off onto side roads, pulled over; the stress unbearable, especially if I had been working a hard shift. The situation outside the hairdressers was mentioned to our supervisors, who made ridiculous comments we should report Mr Bates and the Little fella for public order offences or minor road traffic offences. Was I willing to put myself on a pedestal, so they might receive a £50 fine after a lengthy trial? Was I fuck!

Myself and Fred put a report into our supervisors, naming the heroin gang and asking for extra support in the area. We met the officer in charge of the station and told him our concerns; to our horror he showed no interest and as we spoke he looked out of the window; not taking much notice. He only commented about the large number of criminals mentioned in our report—'Fuck him,' we both said after the meeting, 'Thousands of coppers in this force, and it's just a couple to deal with this fucking mess,' I said. After our meeting with the station boss, on my extra-long drive home; Magazine's 'Shot by both sides' played on the car radio, which summed up my week perfectly.

Fred helped whenever he found time, which pleased me because he was the real thing and one of the only coppers I trusted. I booked out an observation van; a normal van with no markings to suggest it belonged to the police. Cockney J wasn't available, neither was Fred, so I begged a detective new to the area to drive, whilst I filmed out of the rear window. I instructed him to drive to a garage where I knew the gang associated. When we got there, I saw the Little fella and Mr Bates talking to another male, as we got closer, I could not believe my eyes—they were only talking and laughing with the local area bobby; then like in the movies, passed him a brown parcel. The detective, worried they had spotted him, in a panic sped off, driving into a dead end street. His tension increased and he slammed the brakes on, throwing me about in the back of the van, almost knocking me out. If they hadn't seen him before; they had now.

We drove back to the police station, and I informed the station boss what I had witnessed; I was warned to keep it quiet. I got more concerned by the day; the local bobby regularly came into the drug unit office, asking how things were going and not having a proper conversation, just being a nosey bastard. I didn't know him well, but knew he was due to retire. Other officers named him the Peeping Tom because when he was on foot patrol, he followed drunken courting couples home and peeped through their curtains, hoping to catch them in a sexual act.

Not long after witnessing him receiving the brown package, Peeping Tom resigned, taking early retirement, and went to work for a local security firm run by a city gangster. He should have gone to prison in my eyes and my paranoia became unbearable. I was given permission to take my police radio home, to inform the local police if my home was under attack. This didn't comfort me, as I went to bed each night with hammers and knives under my pillow. I also kept a few weapons near to my front door and planned over and over how to attack anybody who might come through my door.

Kath questioned me about my behaviour and I brought her up-to-date with the growing situation. She became stressed and packed her job in at a bank which was near to the tower-block estate. I felt worthless, as she took a ten-inch knife to bed each night, kept under her pillow, and now she didn't have a job to go to. One-night Kath woke me up by pressing the knife against my throat; she had been having nightmares. We then received several silent phone calls a day, and when my children answered the phone, the caller asked if their dad was there; once the phone was handed over to me the line went dead. My home telephone number was ex-directory, but it later came to light that the gang had recruited a British Telecom engineer to work for them, a person who would play a big part in a serious crime.

I wasn't listening to music at this time, but Joy Divisions' 'Digital' track would have suited the situation nicely. It didn't seem fair, at any moment criminals might come through my front door with machetes and guns. My mind told me to protect my home, this meant fighting fire with fire and purchasing a gun. Thoughts crossed my mind if I should use my criminal contacts to purchase one, and I wouldn't have hesitated in shooting anyone who intended to hurt my family. But this would have also destroyed my family, because I would lose my job and go to prison. I was in a bad way, and even had intrusive thoughts about humanely killing my wife and children so they couldn't be tortured and murdered by the gang. I'd then be free to go to war with the young firm, and not have to worry about the consequences; these thoughts created an enormous and truly ugly fish in my bag. My mind was fucking me up, and the thought of my supervisor looking out of his window hurt. I was in my own mental war zone; but I didn't have an army alongside me, I had no people I could trust or rely on, I didn't have any guns and I had two small children to care for, all whilst trying to live and work in such a dark, dark place.

About a week before Christmas, I was sitting in the drugs unit office researching a job, when Fred stumbled in. His skin looked a grey colour and he appeared shaken. Without hesitation I asked him if he was okay and he told me that whilst driving around the tower block estate, the Little fella and Mr Bates waved him down. They then ran over to his car and dragged him out of it, before attempting to force him into their vehicle; Fred struggled and escaped. At the time I could only imagine what they planned for him—but soon found out what their intentions may have been.

Not long after this incident, Fred moved away from the city to the national crime squad; not being a detective constable like Fred I had less of an opportunity to get away. Fred knew the attempted kidnapping of him would never be proven, so I don't believe it was investigated. The rest of Christmas 1998 was quiet, and apart from the usual drugs warrants for amphetamines and cannabis, there seemed little movement on the streets. Amongst all the chaos, I tried to make sure my wife and children enjoyed their Christmas.

I realised 1999 would be as violent as 1998. Although the streets were quiet, I stood on top of a simmering volcano, which at any moment could erupt. In February 1999, I submitted another report to my supervision, naming the gang, their activities, and asking for extra support. The report named the

Big fella, the Little fella and Mr Bates. The Red Indian had been remanded in prison for chopping a dealer to bits; the Knife, convicted of murder. Mr Clever was awaiting trial for the drugs offence, so he kept his nose clean, and I hadn't seen or heard of Rupert the Bear for months. The report also mentioned ten local lads who ran the drugs for the gang.

As a result, our supervision instructed a few reluctant detectives to take a look at the gang. Shortly after submitting the report, I was in the drugs unit when a detective barged in. Excitedly he told us to be very careful, as he had received information that the Little fella owned a Mac 10 machine gun, and he could kill an officer. I buried my head in my hands before telling him I had submitted these intelligence reports months previously, and I now knew nothing had been done with them!

Then in March an office meeting was arranged and to my utter surprise, I heard something I could not comprehend. Myself, Cockney J and the proactive unit were told the drugs unit and the proactive unit were being disbanded. We needed to put a report in to our supervision, stating where we wanted to go. There wasn't a 'thank you,' 'kiss my arse,' or anything for the work we had done, just—get back to uniform. I put a report into my supervision asking to be transferred to another part of the city; away from areas where I had patrolled and studied the young firm. The report was returned, informing me I would be in uniform—driving a police van around the tower block area! I got the feeling my supervision didn't give a shit or didn't understand, and they might as well have put a target on the back of my uniform.

At the end of March, I was deployed to assist in arresting criminals who were identified in a massive undercover operation. The operation ran for several months in the city, and because of its secrecy, only a selected few knew it existed. Was somebody investigating the young firm after all? At the end of the arrest stage of the operation, the headlines in the local paper read, 'Swoop on the untouchables,' fifty-nine criminals had been arrested for a variety of offences. I studied the list of people arrested, and even though the operation was fantastic and great PR for the city—not one young firm member had been arrested.

The untouchables had not been touched, which left me gutted. At the beginning of April, I patrolled around the tower block estate looking for the young firm's drug runners. But it wasn't easy in a big marked police van. The runners would laugh, saying I must have fucked up to be demoted back to uniform, they also found it necessary to continue with the graffiti abuse. The criminals thought being in the drugs unit and working in plain clothes was a promotion; but some cops did. Also in April, I attended Crown Court to watch Mr Clever and The Bolt pleading guilty for the drug offences. They received lengthy sentences.

It was rumoured that when the Prime minister disappeared, his associates thought it natural to take over. This annoyed a member of the young firm who was receiving payments from the Prime Minister for time he spent in custody on a kidnap charge. He must have kept his mouth shut, so as not to implicate the Prime Minister or one of his associates in the crime; but this payment stopped once the Prime Minister went on the run. The young firm approached the close associates of the Prime Minister asking for the payments which they should have been receiving. When they refused to pay the money, the Big fella threatened to kill them. The once strong gang covering the whole of this city found itself fractured beyond belief.

In April an unknown offender shot at a security guard on a demolition site situated near to the petrol station estate and owned by the Big fella. Nobody came forward to identify the gunman or the security guard, but something appeared to be developing. It was believed the associates of the Prime Minister used the firearm as a warning to the Big fella, after he had threatened to kill them. With nobody murdered or seriously injured the local detectives investigated the incident, but as no one would speak to the police, there were no lines of enquiry and the crime was filed undetected. In retaliation, the Big fellas' gang travelled out of the city, kidnapped a male and tortured him, attempting to obtain the whereabouts of the people responsible for shooting at the security guard. The violence spiralled out of control.

At the end of April, reports of a shooting at a public house in the tower-block area came over the police radio. It soon became common knowledge that the Big fella had been shot several times by a masked gunman. Most people thought he would have died, but amazingly after a few days he walked out of hospital with a bullet still inside him. Selfishly, I was happy the gang had something else to concentrate on now instead of me; and concentrate they did!

The Big fella knew who had tried to kill him: the same people his gang had been putting pressure on—he wanted revenge. The young firm couldn't find the people responsible for shooting the Big fella, so they would go to work on their associates. Unbeknown to a British telecom sales manager, the gang were going to become his worst nightmare. The sales manager was a part-time bouncer at a pub in a town 15 miles away from the tower-block area. Another bouncer who worked the doors with him asked the BT man to do him a little favour; this bouncer was associated to the young firm. Thinking it was probably a 'one off' and maybe to impress the city bouncer, the BT man did the little favour, which was a big mistake. The city bouncer informed the young firm about his 'tame' BT friend, and now it would be the young firm asking him to do a little favour for them.

One night, while at home with his family, the gang paid the BT man a visit. At first the young firm asked him to obtain a few addresses from telephone numbers they had gathered whilst torturing people. He refused to help, but the young firm reminded him that he had already passed on information to their bouncer friend which on its own could get him sacked. The politeness then wore off, and in front of the BT man's family, he was viciously assaulted by the gang, who also smashed the windows to his family home. They threatened if he went to the police, they would harm his family. Within a short time, the BT bouncer found himself in a very lonely place, and fearing for the life of himself and his family. What else could he do? He probably regretted the day he ever spoke to his mate, the city bouncer. Under duress, the BT man faxed the addresses which the young firm had requested, and the young firm booked themselves into a hotel to plan their next moves. The BT man would later be arrested for his actions and during the police interview he shed tears.

Still seriously injured, The Big fella went to war with the people who had attempted to kill him. His generals the Little fella and Mr Bates were in charge of the operation. Armed with personal details provided by the BT man, the young firm kidnapped and tortured two men, then attempted to kidnap another.

The kidnaps and shootings ended with 11 of the young firm charged, convicted and imprisoned. Reporters would later accurately inform the public about the kidnappings from behind their desks.

The first kidnapping took place two miles away from my home address; the male occupant was shot and kidnapped in front of his girlfriend. I now wondered if the extra help I had requested would now be made available. It also crossed my mind why I should give a toss, because it was the boss's choice to get rid of the drugs unit and put me back in uniform. However, I still had death threats to worry about and wondered if I featured on the young firm's hit list. The only positive thought which crossed my mind, was they would be far more interested in people that had tried to kill them, than someone responsible for arresting their dealers. Still, I wasn't prepared to take any chances.

Horror of gang's orgy of torture and kidnapping

The young firm drove the first kidnap victim to an old caravan, kept on farmland close to where he lived, and in an attempt to find out the whereabouts of the people responsible for shooting the Big fella, the young firm tortured him. A few days later, another man was shot and kidnapped from his home address. Both kidnap victims were interrogated by the young firm, but didn't know the details the young firm needed. The gang wanted something for all their hard work, so they made the first man phone his family and associates requesting £50,000 for his release; after many phone calls, he only raised £10,500. I thought, 'do his associates not have the cash, or do they not give a fuck about him?' The gang shot and tried to kidnap a third male; he escaped and ended up on armed guard at the hospital. I spent a few days looking after him at the hospital, but he refused to speak. This criminal lived in the tower-block area and I had a few previous dealings with him, which weren't pleasant.

After the kidnappings and ransom bid, it surprised me how many resources were now made available to catch the gang. The national crime squad made an appearance; a major incident room was created, and detectives got brought in from all across the force. The second victim ended up being dumped near the hospital, only because the gang thought he was going to die. The first victim escaped, leaving the young firm nobody left to barter with.

Prior to losing their captives, the gang threatened their two victims, telling them to lie to the police by saying the criminals who had kidnapped them, were the same people who had tried to kill the Big fella. Then once the police arrested these criminals, the young firm would be able to kill them from inside prison. This never happened, and seemed a bizarre request—maybe the gang had run out of ideas?

To my surprise, because of my local knowledge of the gang, I was asked to join the major incident room. At first I felt like telling them to piss off, but I wanted to see how the big boys worked. The Detective Sergeant running the incident room was switched-on, and within a few months the gang had been rounded up, arrested and charged. Firearms were recovered and deals were made. Investigating officers found police reports and intelligence in some of the offenders' addresses, proving an officer was working for them. They also found the victims' addresses which had been faxed through by the BT man. As far as I'm aware the officer, or officers, could not be traced through the paperwork.

I later attended Crown Court with the Detective Sergeant and looked at the dock which had most of the young firm lined up—the same lads I watched leaving the pub the year before. Only a small partition divided them from the public; which concerned me. The Big fella was given a life sentence; the Little fella and Mr Bates were both given a lengthy sentence and the rest of the gang also received quite long sentences. The Little fellas' girlfriend was also sentenced for trying to bribe witnesses into not giving evidence against the young firm.

In November 2000, the Red Indian who had been in prison at the time of the kidnappings, was shot to death within the tower-block area, believed to be over something trivial.

At the beginning of 2001, I started as a trainee detective; but after about eight weeks I quit the course. I didn't trust any of the people in the CID, and the Chief Inspector wasn't the most helpful person I had ever met. Criminals continued working for the young firm, and as far as I knew, so did police officers. I still drove home using different routes and felt like my brain was on fire.

Cold-blooded killing

Never in my life had I ever felt so low and requested to go back on uniformed patrol. From this moment, I knew I wouldn't be offered another opportunity in this city. On uniformed patrol my mood swings were obviously pissing off my colleagues, but I couldn't prevent myself from feeling this way. A colleague described me as being the most paranoid person he had ever met in his life.

Then one evening I was on patrol with this officer, and behind one of the tower blocks I saw the moon—the largest moon I had ever seen! I could have reached out and touched it. The thought rushed, 'What the fuck is this life about? This can't be all there is?'

I drove back to the station and my intention was to hand in my warrant card, and walk away from the police service, which was making me so miserable. Just before handing my warrant card in, I thought of my wife and children and realised it was my responsibility to support them. So rather than quit my job, I did an act I thought I'd never do; I asked my supervision to book me an appointment with the occupational health unit. If quitting CID was not enough, being referred to the occupational health would definitely mark my cards as being a failure in the cops. It was my last chance though, and I didn't have a clue what to expect.

At the start of April 2002 I visited the occupational health department, and spoke to a welfare officer who seemed to be very kind, I hadn't met this type of caring person before in my life. He diagnosed me as having an acute stress reaction caused by the work I had been involved in. A report was sent to the Superintendent on the division I was working on, and within weeks I received a message on my scratch pad telling me to start on a new division covering a working class town; closer to where I lived, but still adjoining the division where I was working.

I received no further help or support from the occupational health department, which would come back and bite me on my arse years later; nobody from the division I was working on spoke to me about my move. It was just a case of move, and let's see how it works out. I emptied the contents of my locker into a cardboard box and placed the box into the boot of my car. Shaking my head, I drove away from the Victorian building. It was time for a new start....

Chapter six

Out of the city

The human resources department gave me the name of my new division by leaving a message on my scratchpad—a division is just another town or city. I received no communication from anyone at my old station, or occupational health. It felt as though my first 9 years working for the police hadn't happened, but the memories of working there still lingered in my mind.

My new division covered a rundown working-class town, which had been active during the Industrial Age. I knew this town, because it was where I first worked as an apprentice engineer. On my first day I entered the police station and spoke to the Sergeant in charge of my shift. 'I believe you're here because you thumped the Superintendent,' he quizzed me.

'You can believe what you want, I'm only here to work, is that okay?' I replied. I'd gone against the police system, and somebody wanted to make life difficult for me.

I left the Sergeant's office and walked into the locker room to change into my uniform. As I entered the room, the first person I saw was an old colleague from the city division. He was banging his head forcibly into his locker. I said hello—he turned and through gritted teeth said; 'I need to get out of this fucking job.' He told me he always banged his head against his locker before starting his shift. I didn't ask why.

I entered the parade room and saw a new group of officers. These were the townie cops that had never worked in a city, a different breed of police officers. I looked around the parade table and there was a hierarchy; the police constable in charge was a policewoman who other officers gave the name 'Effing Lisa,' because every other word out of her mouth was 'Fucking.' She was an older officer from Yorkshire and looked very similar to Wee Jimmy Krankie. I looked at her as she sat with her hands behind her head, showing everybody the yellow stained armpits of her white shirt. I had a bad feeling about this officer and I later found out the integrity unit investigated her for being 'too close' to the criminals. The Sergeant then told me I should spend a month on the van with 'Effing Lisa,' and after this month on patrol my thoughts didn't change about her one bit. She did not last long in the police and went living back in Yorkshire with a criminal, who she had befriended whilst working in Manchester.

Although the town wasn't as violent as the city, it was surprisingly busy because every member of the public wanted to tell the police everything. From working in a place where nobody would grass, I was now working in a town full of informants!

One of the first incidents with my new colleagues was a report of a man threatening people with an axe. I approached the offender's address with another officer, who would later be given the name

'Faster than Facebook,' because he was always gossiping. As we approached the house, the man came out waving the axe, without thinking we dove at him before he took control and buried the axe in our heads. We spent a few minutes rolling around in the dog shit on his front lawn before 'Faster than Facebook' assisted by spraying me full in the face with his CS gas! This incident gave other officers confidence in me, which always helped a new officer.

Not long after I had been working on this new division, I received a letter asking me to attend the force headquarters to receive an award from the Chief Constable for the work I had done on the shooting and kidnapping enquiry. He would hand me the award, have a photo opportunity and the press would make a big show of it all. I sent the letter back asking them to send the award through the post. Although I didn't want the pomp and glory bullshit, an award from the top cop was always handy if I ever got in the shit. The framed commendation arrived and I took it home and placed it under my bed. The last thing I wanted a burglar to see if they broke into my house was a police award pinned up on my wall.

After six months in this outer station, the bosses moved me to the divisional headquarters. It wasn't my choice; but one thing I found throughout my time in the cops, was every new boss wanted to change the way the police worked to justify their position. They moved officers so they couldn't settle or become complacent; the worst thing an officer could do was to admit they enjoyed the job. If they did, it wouldn't be long before the bosses pulled rank and moved them. The headquarters produced a bad vibe because it was full of bosses who looked for any excuse to fuck you over.

I wasn't fond of the move, but an opportunity arose to get back into plain clothes and earn a few hours' overtime. I noticed a pattern emerging where a male flashing his penis at the bus station frightened single women and young children to death. It happened each Tuesday night, and as I was on the day shift the following Tuesday, I asked if I could stay on for a few hours. The bosses agreed, so I persuaded a young female probationer to stand on the bus stop platform, waiting to be flashed at.

I hid near the platform and after around an hour of watching, a man shuffled across the bus station with his hood up. He stared at the female probationer until he grabbed her attention, he then pulled out his penis and tugged on it. Upon seeing this I ran across the platform and dove at him; taking him to the floor. When I searched the male inside his coat pocket I found a plastic comic nose similar in shape to a penis. The probationer, shocked at the perverts wanking actions looked away, and couldn't commit herself to saying she saw his penis; so I went to court on my own to give evidence. It became clear the plastic 'penis-shaped' nose would be the pervert's defence, as he told the court that I had seen his comic nose, not his penis. It was now time for 'Exhibit JJ1' — 'Officer, could you please show the magistrates the exhibit you seized from my client's pocket.'

Slowly I lifted the comic plastic nose/penis into the air, which caused all the magistrates to break down in fits of laughter. The defence team had won, and the pervert was found not guilty because the court could not rely on my evidence alone. Luckily he was re-called to prison because he had over one hundred previous convictions of similar offences.

I worked at this station for another 6 months and my new Sergeant was the biggest bully I had seen in the police. He was constantly trying to 'leg' officers. Which meant he would always find things they were doing wrong, then put them on an action plan, and if they didn't improve he would discipline them. He pulled me into his office saying, 'Our team need more prisoners, so get some or I'll put you on an action plan to improve.' I hated his attitude and I would normally do less for a supervisor like this, but not wanting to be 'legged' I arrested anybody I could; within three months I had arrested over 40 people for a variety of offences.

After six months at this station an opportunity arose for me as a proactive officer, working in plain clothes. This proactive unit had been newly formed and would be used to target problem areas, I didn't need much persuasion and applied for the position. After I told them what I had already done in the police, they didn't hesitate to give me the job. I turned up at this new station and Sergeant Harwood who was, and still is completely barking mad, showed me around and bluntly said to me; 'If you're shit, I'll fuck you off.' At least he was being honest.

Sergeant Harwood handpicked all the ten officers in this unit and as the it had been formed by the bosses, they gave us a free reign with what vehicles we wanted, and as long as we got results they protected us. Like any other proactive unit, the variety of the jobs we became involved in was immense; one day we could investigate a spate of burglaries, the next day we may investigate large drug deals.

The first thing I noticed when I came to this town, was nobody knew or cared about the gang structures. After attending and dealing with a few assaults on uniform patrol, I started to understand the structure, which consisted of at least three separate gangs predominantly run by young Asian males. I could not believe officers didn't know which criminals belonged to which gang. The gang members I dealt with were not as violent as the criminals in the city, but their strength in being business-like accumulated them lots of money and power. They also had strength in numbers and many contacts in the drug circles, which gave them a big advantage over the white city gangs.

The testosterone in the proactive unit needed to be channelled; our Sergeant was interested in mountain climbing and fell running and as there was a hillside near to our office; he told us to start work a couple of hours early—at the bottom of a hill! I had played rugby before but I had never run up and down a bloody big hill. None of us had the correct footwear, this became clear when most of us slid down the other side of the hill which was a lot of fun, especially when it was pissing down with rain. If we didn't run, we went to the gym in the station. I even went rock climbing with Sgt Harwood, but I didn't have a head for heights.

I think our Sergeant wanted to create some kind of SAS unit and encouraged a few ex-military officers to join our team; which they jumped at. These years were easily the best time I spent in the police and although we worked very long hours and were exposed to violent members of the public, it was pleasurable. However, this style of policing wasn't everyone's cup of tea, a few higher ranking officers waited for it all to fail, which after a few years it did; spectacularly!

I took it upon myself to start making sense of the Asian gangs, which meant entering their areas and stopping, searching or just speaking to them. I would not describe their areas as ghettos, however white people and especially police officers were not welcome there. Their insults and negative attitude towards me didn't compare to the behaviour displayed by the inner city gangs, so after facing the abuse for a few months I now entered their areas with ease and had no problem communicating with them.

The majority of the Asian criminals possessed a great sense of humour and part of the fun was to provide officers with false names. Most officers couldn't get their heads around these names, which they found difficult to pronounce or spell, so they didn't bother. To get over this obstacle I learned a few phrases in Urdu from a contact within the community. The Asian lads would speak in Urdu around officers; so, it took them by surprise when I asked them their name: 'Aapka naam kya hai?' Shocked at this white copper speaking Urdu, they gave up their name. I would then ask them in Urdu to tell me their real name, which normally made them laugh, unfortunately I only learned enough phrases to bullshit them a little. Most of the gangs drove around in hire cars and always had some kind of weapon with them, mainly knives or baseball bats. Guns were not popular, but did start creeping in when the tension between the gangs mounted.

Unlike the city division, heroin and crack cocaine proved to be a massive industry in this town. Drug deals were organised by the Asian gangs, who generally employed white heroin addicts or immigrants to do the drug dealing for them. The gangs would let the addicts run up a debt which they could never pay back, so rather than being assaulted, they agreed to sell drugs to pay it off. The gangs provided the dealers with a hire vehicle and gave them a list of users who they had to deal the heroin and crack to. The dealers' working hours were normally between 10am and 10pm; they received no money but kept a couple of bags of heroin as payment.

A trick the gangs used was to wait until the addict parked up the hire vehicle at night and when the addicts slept, the gang smashed the windows of the hire vehicle. The addicts would report this to the gang the following morning, only to be told they needed to work longer hours to pay for the damage. It was a vicious circle and most of the dealers seemed glad to be arrested.

Next to the proactive office was another office which contained the drugs unit. The officers in this unit, although experienced, didn't have a clue what was going on and only produced results by using information provided by informants. Our office, like its name suggested, was more proactive; we generated our own workload by trawling the streets looking for criminals. The drugs unit weren't that interested, so our unit could also look at drug dealers. Unlike the city division I had previously worked in, this town was full of drug dealers and addicts; the town looked like a zombie film, with addicts shuffling around, waiting for their next fix.

One night I drove near to an outside market area, just across the road from a police station. It wasn't hard to spot a few addicts, who gathered under one of the stalls. It was dark and pissing down, and because the view wasn't the best from my car I got out and waited at a bus stop nearby. After a few minutes a male arrived on a bicycle and rode towards the group, who became fidgety with excitement. I could see the male wore a rucksack on his back, with what appeared to be a pole sticking out of the top of it. I radioed to other officers to close in on the group who had surrounded the cyclist; I then witnessed exchanges being made. After the last exchange, I walked towards the male on the bike, and as he cycled away; I pounced on him, knocking him from his bike and pinning him to the floor. Other officers assisted, and upon searching his rucksack, we found 40 wraps of heroin and 40 wraps of crack cocaine, and what had appeared to be a pole protruding from his rucksack, turned out to be a samurai sword. Fortunately, he hadn't been given the chance to use the weapon.

Sgt Harwood, over the moon with this arrest, made me the 'man of the match.' This was going to be easy, with dealers all over the town it wouldn't require much effort to catch them and send them to prison for at least three years. It was 'sexy policing' to catch a drug dealer carrying such an intimidating weapon but I found out weeks later, carrying an offensive weapon without possessing drugs wasn't as sexy.

I received information drug dealing was happening in a local park, and as a result of this information, myself and another officer dressed ourselves in plain clothes and walked through the park to see if the information was correct.

Upon entering the park, a male in his twenties walked in our direction and appeared to be exiting the park. As we crossed, the male angrily said; 'What the fuck are you looking at?' He then reached inside his jacket, pulled out a machete and waved it in front of our faces.

In situations like this you either think about it, or act without worrying about the consequences;

luckily for us we didn't ponder and within a split second we had pinned the lad to the floor, taking the machete from his grasp. This lad had previous convictions for breaking a stranger's jaw during a bus journey and many other assaults, so it surprised me when after I'd interviewed him, the Sergeant in the custody office bailed him. This meant he left the station, but would have to attend Magistrates' court a few weeks later. This really pissed me off, as we had arrested a dangerous man willing to wave a machete at strangers in a public place—and he was free. I stayed for a few hours after my shift had finished, completing the paperwork. This was the first time I realised the system was totally knackered. In my opinion he should have gone straight to prison.

'I had nothing to keep him in for,' said the Sergeant.

'How about this, Sergeant—he's a dangerous bastard who could chop somebody's head off,' I replied in frustration. But it was no use, by this time the lad was probably at home having his tea.

As the unit was extremely busy and having nobody to hand our prisoners over to, I worked lots of overtime which paid for a family holiday in Majorca for a week. I was over the moon to be taking my family to Spain. The first day after arriving, we happily skipped down towards the beach with our buckets and spades; as I looked further down the street, I couldn't believe what I saw! Walking towards us was Mr Clever, who belonged to the inner city drugs gang. Before he clocked me, I bundled my wife and two daughters into a shop, telling them not to ask questions. I peeped through the Lillo's and watched as Mr Clever walked past the shop. This was all I needed, he wouldn't think twice of inflicting violence; if my kids were there or not. All week the hyper-vigilance kicked in—watching everybody. I spotted Mr Clever a few more times and avoided him, which was hard to do with two children in tow. Maybe he was enjoying a deserved break after his prison sentence? I spent a few days of my holiday in bed, coughing blood. Could it be a dodgy kebab or pure nerves? I got through the week and my children had a nice break, but I was glad when I got back home and even back to work.

As a unit we always patrolled the streets, I worked out the gang structure in the town, which consisted of three main gangs and a few up-and-coming ones. Two of the gangs or as the bosses preferred to call them, organised crime groups, were predominantly made up of young Pakistani males and lived about two miles from each other—they went by the names the Bromwich and the Queens gangs. The other gang was the Torvill gang, who were young Indian males, smaller in number than the Pakistani gangs, but they stuck together in any situation and hated the Queens gang with a passion. I first got to know the Torvill and the Queens gang on uniformed patrol. I had received a radio message about a group of Asian men with knives and baseball bats, fighting in the street.

I drove to the area and could see the fighting had stopped; I also noticed a few lads surrounding another male, who lay on the floor, covered in blood.

In usual townie style, every one of them wanted to give me a statement. The lad on the floor, who I called Crystal, was the leader of the Torvill gang and had been struck around the head with baseball bats by members of the Queens gang. I took several statements and attended the address where three of the Queens gang lived with their parents. As I entered the address, I came across two of the gang responsible for attacking Crystal. After arresting them they couldn't wait to inform me their uncle was a police inspector—in the area I worked! I didn't know this Inspector, but a few years later he ended up in prison for some dodgy mortgage transactions.

The Queens lads didn't try to run or put up a fight, they also surprisingly parked their vehicle around the back of their house. Witnesses had described this vehicle and when I looked inside it, I found a load of baseball bats; I could not believe how easy the Queens lads had made it for me. I was still investigating this crime when I began working within the proactive unit, so I was in the right position to study the gang structure when it all got messy. Obviously, the Torvill lads weren't going to forget the assault on their leader, and a few more fights occurred in pubs and clubs between them and the Queens lads.

One night I was patrolling with another officer, driving an unmarked car around the Queens area, when we heard over our radio there had been a drive-by shooting in the area. I attended this area, and it became clear someone had shot at the Torvill lads, all because they ventured into the Queens area. This was a step up from fighting with knives and sticks and suddenly the bosses in the police station took notice. To me, they still played at being gangsters, because the criminals in the inner-city wouldn't have just fired a warning shot; they would have killed them. Even so, firing a gun on a British street was a serious offence, and one not to go ignored.

I had recruited a few informants and one of them told me the Torvill lads were arming themselves; an informant told me they kept their stash in a car which they parked near to Crystal's address. Our unit spent over a month following and observing the Queens gang. On one occasion, which was the hottest day of the year, I was in the back of an observation van with another officer who looked similar to Shrek. Within five minutes of being in back of the van, which had no ventilation, we found ourselves stripped naked, down to our boxer shorts. Condensation dripped off the ceiling like raindrops and before long, both of us were physically sick. The lad we watched was the shooter who fired the gun at the Torvill lads; we couldn't be removed for the plot, so we had to grin and bear it. Fourteen hours later, there had been no movement. By this time, the temperature had dropped—we both shivered and had banging headaches, wearing our wet clothes we had put back on.

I spent many hours watching criminals from the rear of an observation van, but I never came so close to dying in the back of one as I had on this occasion. Eventually the suspect came out of his address and I could send a message through to the firearms team, who arrested him nearby. Even after this message, it was another hour and a half before we got removed from the plot. The Sergeant running the operation apologised to us, but I don't think he gave a toss, as long as he got a result. The public don't understand what some officers put themselves through to catch criminals; I wish they could spend just one day in the back of an observation van, having to piss in a bottle and sometimes having to crap in a bag. Then if it was boiling, they could inhale their own piss and shit, or even worse; their mate's piss and shit.

With most of the Queens lads on remand in prison, the next target would be the Torvill gang. Before this though I was to take my wife and two children on a well-deserved week's holiday to Ibiza and hoped it would be more relaxing than the one I spent looking out for Mr Clever. It had been twelve months since my holiday with Mr Clever, so we tried somewhere different and ended up going to Ibiza for a week. It was a fantastic holiday, and we all enjoyed our time there. After the holiday had finished, a coach dropped us off at the airport. When they called for the passengers to board the plane, we strolled to the check-in and being so relaxed, we were the last people on the shuttle bus, which would transport us from the check-in to our plane.

As I was looking at the plane ahead of me, I felt the atmosphere on the bus change. The holidaymakers on the shuttle bus appeared tense. I looked at the passengers and noticed dread on their faces. I turned my head to see the cause of the tension; five Asian teenagers, all with rucksacks on their backs ran towards our shuttle bus and boarded it before it set off—as they did, the white passengers looked scared to death but didn't utter a word. This wasn't long after the 9/11 terrorist attacks, and I could understand why the passengers were concerned until I took a closer look at the lads; to my surprise I saw they were all members of the Torvill gang. I couldn't believe it—my only concern was they would give me some lip. The white passengers, however, must have thought they would be blown to bits. What didn't help was when we boarded the plane, the song 'If I saw you in heaven,' sung by Eric Clapton, played on the aircraft radio. I chuckled to myself and prevented being spotted by the Torvill lads for the rest of the flight. A large amount of calls came into the police control room around this time, normally along the lines of; 'There's an Asian male with a rucksack, and he is looking very nervous.' I wasn't surprised he was nervous; every white person was staring at him!

On my return to work, I saw that the Torvill gang had now started to throw their weight around.

The break must have done them good. An informant told me they had gained in confidence since the arrest of the Queens gang and had now got hold of some firearms of their own. With this information and the fact that our bosses didn't want another firearms incident on their patch, our instructions consisted of breaking down the Torvill gang. After getting to know them from investigating the assault on Crystal, I didn't have any problem spending time chatting to them within their territory. They also thought I supported them because we had removed the Queens gang from the streets.

I received information that the Torvill gang had a stash in the rear of a motor vehicle. Our unit got several search warrants so we could enter the Torvill lads' houses to search for weapons and drugs. The house I was interested in was Crystal's; he lived at this address with his two brothers, also in the gang, and his mother. As we entered and started the search, Crystal was over-friendly towards me, and happy for us to search his house, because he knew there was nothing in there. What interested me more though was a large bunch of car keys in his living room. I asked the family about the car keys and they tried to deflect the question. Little did they know I had already been informed that the gang's stash was stored in a car which they parked near to Crystal's home address. I checked all the cars on the terraced street and when a Ford Focus came back as having a registered keeper in Liverpool, I looked for a Ford key amongst the bunch of keys. After trying a few keys, I found the key which opened the Ford. I opened the boot and bingo! There it was, the Torvill gang's stash, a boot containing about £50,000 worth of cocaine, lots of ammunition and other weapons, including their favourite baseball bats.

I arrested Crystal and his two brothers for drugs and firearms offences. Other members of the gang were also arrested after finding drugs and weapons at their addresses. When I interviewed Crystal, I couldn't help but mentioning I knew he had been on a certain plane, at a certain time. Upon hearing this, he stared at me saying 'How the fuck do you know?' He must have thought the FBI had been following him all over the world. I didn't have the heart to tell him we holidayed in the same resort. Crystal and his gang were linked to the stash and given lengthy custodial sentences. A fantastic result!

With both the Queens and Torvill gangs removed from the gang scene, this only left the Bromwich gang, who proved to be more difficult to catch. They were very anti-police and a close-knit gang, but it wasn't long before they destroyed themselves following the brutal murder of a relative of the Queens gang. The main players in the Bromwich gang were arrested for this murder; or they fled the country to evade arrest, which meant that the Bromwich gang also ceased to exist. With the three main gangs now gone, the gang violence in the town was no longer an issue.

As we took control of the gang violence, we now had more time to deal with other criminal offences. One day I was out in a plain vehicle with two lads, one I called 'Marine' because he served in the Paratroopers and he hated the marines, the other lad I called 'Joe' because he looked like the comedian Joe Pasquale. An unusual amount of house burglaries occurred in one of the nicer areas of the town, and because the bosses' figures were rising, they had asked our unit to have a look at who was committing the burglaries. As we drove down a street in this area, we noticed a male stood next to a parked car; call it judgemental but we all knew by looking at him, he had never passed his driving test. I thought he had either broken into the car or was going to nick it, until he lifted a safe from the back seat of the car. We pulled up near to the car and even though we were in an unmarked car and in plain clothes, the male recognized us as being police officers. As he did, he threw the safe back in the car and jumped into the driver's seat. Before he had the chance to shut the driver's door, I pounced on him and leaned into the car, wrapping my arms around his neck and waist. In a desperate attempt to get away, he threatened me with a knife but as I had his arms semi-pinned to his body, he couldn't raise the knife. He did somehow start the engine of the car and to my horror, the car moved forward. I had two choices, let go, or go for a ride, and for some reason I chose the second option. After running for a short distance: I was dragged alongside the car. If I was to release at this point, I would have gone under the rear wheels so I lovingly squeezed onto my new best mate. After about 50 feet, the speed of the car was increasing, and I felt in serious danger, using my upper body I pulled at the male and we both popped out of the car like a champagne cork, landing on the tarmac road. My colleagues ran to help and handcuffed the male. I couldn't move my body, my lower back had been damaged as we twisted and fell. As I lay on the road, I saw the empty car which I had just been in, continue on its own up the road before crashing into somebody's garden fence. The ambulance took me to the hospital where I received treatment for the damage to the muscles and nerves in my back. I lay on the hospital bed, glad of the rest and thinking to myself how lucky I had been.

The male later admitted to numerous burglaries in the area, and because of his arrest, the burglary figures went down. I was off work injured; and to be fair to the bosses on this occasion, they phoned asking about my welfare. The lads in the unit also bought flowers for my wife, for putting up with me. The team spirit in this unit made going to work very pleasurable. Unfortunately, these times rarely happen in the police. I attended court to give evidence on this case, and during the summing up of the case the Judge commended me for my actions; he later sent me a framed certificate, which I put under my bed. A judge's commendation was another 'get out of jail free' card if I got in the shit. To top it off, I met the Chief Constable, who gave me a Chief Constable commendation for bravery. An officer who was organising the ceremony whispered, 'You're fucking milking this one, mate.' I laughed because I was, but it was a morning away from work and I possessed another 'get out of jail free' card to put under my bed.

After a few weeks of returning to work, the police advertised, asking officers if they would be interested in applying to be undercover officers. The course they advertised was the undercover officer foundation course, low level undercover work, buying crack and heroin from drug dealers and associating with what some people would class as low-lives, the lowest of the low in fact. These undercover officers had been known as TPO's or test purchase officers, but as drug users didn't queue up at a phone box anymore, and the dealers knew the tactics TPO's used, officers needed to take more risks, which meant more planning was required. Myself and another officer called Wellington from my division applied for the course. Wellington looked like a piece of shit; but in my eyes, I was a 'normalish' looking male.

I was also 40 years-old with a family and wondered why I had applied for this course. I mustn't have been thinking straight, however, I applied and was going to give it a go. I saw it as another challenge. Prior to the course starting, Wellington and myself did our homework, we questioned every addict we could: about drug prices, drug terminology and how they could spot a copper. We gained a lot of information for the price of a few bags of chips, and the best advice came from one lad; 'all the cops I know are too cock-sure' he advised.

I listened to the cops in the station and realised how cock-sure they were. Even though I hadn't been an angel growing up, I had been a cop for 14 years and must have picked up some bad habits. Every time a cop said a comment, which only cops said, I noted it. If I passed the course and ended up trying to convince dealers I was a heroin addict, I needed to make sure I didn't slip up with any of these cop sayings, or else the operation would be discontinued, or even worse I could be seriously assaulted. If, as an undercover officer, you asked somebody their address instead of where they lived; or their date of birth instead of when were they born, alarm bells would ring with the criminals, so it was important not to slip-up.

The deceit started as soon as we passed the interview and were accepted to go on the course; I needed to lie to colleagues about being accepted for the undercover course. If we shouted our mouths off regarding the course, we would fail it before it started. The people running the course warned us they had a lot of contacts and word would soon get back to them.

The first day of the course arrived and I wondered what I had let myself in for. All the successful applicants for the course were taken to a classroom; and in true classroom style, all fifteen applicants sat in a semi-circle listening to the trainer, different to any previous trainer they had encountered. An instruction before the course was to create our own identity, which needed to have no link to the cops. We had to know drug terminology and current drug prices, which we were all questioned about. Early on during the course, every student would be interrogated by an experienced undercover officer. One or two officers fell to pieces when pushed by the officer, they couldn't believe somebody spoke to them as though they were a piece of shit on the bottom of the trainers' shoe.

It was clear to see the officers who struggled because after they returned from the interrogation they looked stunned and for some strange reason swore aloud, when they hadn't done before. At the end of the first day, two officers asked to leave the course saying it wasn't for them. The rest of the course proved to be just as challenging, resulting in more officers dropping out. At the end of the course, myself, Wellington and a lad I called Ian, because of his love for The Stone Roses 'Ian Brown', passed the whole course and were deemed suitable to be released onto the streets. It was the most rewarding course I've attended. The full-time undercover officers and the trainers were amazing and this seemed to be part of policing just down my street. But I realised, all I had done is pass a course run by police in a safe environment, even though the trainers didn't come across as police officers I knew they were. I also knew, at any moment after I completed the course I could get a phone call; asking for my availability. It wasn't long before I got that call...

Chapter seven

White rats

A few weeks after completing the course, I received a phone call from Desperate Dan, a Sergeant who supervised the undercover officers.

'How do you fancy doing a job for us?' he asked. I don't know why, but my heart raced; this would be the real thing and I was unsure if I could cut it.

'But I've got a suntan,' I told him, hoping he would think I would be too healthy looking to be an addict and ask someone else instead.

'That's okay, it will only start in a few weeks' time, I'll meet up with you then.'

'Erm.... okay,' I replied as the phone call came to an end. I looked at my chubby glowing healthy face in a nearby mirror and thought to myself; 'Fuck, fuck, fuck, what the fuck have I done?'

Que the theme from the movie 'Rocky,' but replace 'getting stronger' with 'getting skanky.' I had to become a skanky looking piece of shit, but it would not happen without hard work. Like an actor getting ready for a part in a movie, I needed to prepare myself for the task ahead. The big difference was; I would be in real life scenarios where one mistake could cost me dearly. Between the phone call and my first meeting with the undercover team, I needed to get to work. This was before beards became fashionable in 2014, and so to help me with my disguise I grew a full beard, and as it grew I realised this uneven scraggly piece of hair on my face would be my saviour for the time-being. I rose early before work each morning leaving the house for a long run. A wash with soap would have ruined my image, so I cleansed in just water. Some officers on the course splashed on expensive aftershave, which didn't please the trainers. With a diet of pot noodles and crisps, along with 20 fags a day; I achieved the required look. My hair grew wavy in the style of a wild Irishman, this style if left unwashed would complete my image. The suntan faded, leaving me having a 'shit head' dirty sun tan look. My finger nails grew to an ugly length and looked even creepier with dirt underneath them—I now felt comfortable.

I was always a scruffy person but I still needed to dress down a little. The 3-striped Adidas tracksuit bottoms and the dark walking jacket looked great on my course, so I dug them out of the shed. After the course finished, I wrapped them in a plastic bag along with a drop of milk. The milk, now dried, produced the desired smell, and as I ripped open the bag; the stench almost made me vomit—which pleased me. The underwear and the socks smelt as bad and needed to, because if a drug dealer suspected I was a cop, they might strip me to see if I was wearing recording equipment. This never happened, but trust me, they would have puked if they would have done. The walking jacket possessed an internal pocket, where I could hold my wallet, which was an empty packet of rolling tobacco and contained all the drug dealers telephone numbers, scribbled on ripped up fag packets using a small pen I acquired from the bookies. I also possessed silver foil, used by addicts to smoke heroin. Many heroin users I met looked down their noses at other heroin users who injected the drug and some who injected pretended they only smoked it, so people wouldn't think the worst of them. I felt the need to tell my wife and children why there was a sudden change in my appearance; so I told my wife I was in a competition in work, who could grow the longest beard for charity. Pity there wasn't a 'Movember' charity yet, it would have been so much easier explaining why I'd grown the beard. Not that it bothered Kath much; she just complained; 'It's like sleeping with a fucking rapist!'

The story of 'me' was becoming more fucked up. I needed to create a new identity which if challenged, would convince the questioner he was the genuine thing. I also needed to convince myself of the new me which was a difficult task, and to top it off my identity of being a police officer had to disappear. If this little cop person in my head should appear when I was trying to buy drugs, he could ruin the whole job, and put my life at risk. I didn't trust this cop inside me and just kept thinking of ways he would fuck everything up for the new me. So I had to drop all past identities and create this new personal identity. I couldn't mess about; this had to be done accurately if it was to work, the heroin addict had an extremely important role—and the ego loved it.

Introducing Paul......

This imaginary 'me,' had to pass for a convincing addict. He needed a criminal mind, but not a long criminal record; because criminals going through the custody/court procedure will bump into each other, either in the police station, at court or in prison, so criminals knew other criminals. How many addicts did I know who hadn't been arrested multiple times? Not many. I therefore based my identity on the vilest, non-criminal I knew; this was going to be Paul. Paul and his three brothers moved with their father from the tower-block area of the inner city I once worked in. It was part of the inner city 'overflow' which happened at the time. Unfortunately for me and a lot of my mates, they moved near to where we lived.

The four brothers brought their inner-city mentality with them, especially Paul, named 'Bastard Paul' by the local youths. He was a few years older than I and older than most of my mates, who avoided Bastard Paul at all costs to avoid being terrorised by him. To my knowledge, Paul was never arrested, because kids didn't report being kidnapped or assaulted by other kids in the seventies, just like they didn't report being abused by celebrities. So, with my new identity 'Paul' created, I was to become a person I fucking hated and needed to invent a convincing story for this vile human being.

Desperate Dan phoned me once more to give me a date to start the job. On the first morning of the job, I travelled to a remote building in my car and I felt the nerves pounding inside my stomach. This happened every day without fail. My brain would thud; with the story I created for Paul whizzing around inside my head. It was November and the remoteness of the building, on top of a hill with the mist rising, made it feel as though I was walking into a horror movie set. I trudged into the building carrying my black bin bag, containing my clothing and props; the bag tied with a knot to prevent any vital stink from the clothing being lost.

As I walked into the musty smelling building, I observed two local officers looking giddy and excited. These officers would be in charge of arresting anybody who I identified as drug dealers on their division. There was also my welfare officer, employed to look after my wellbeing and as we all introduced ourselves to each other; into the building entered my junkie partner-in-crime—Ian 'fucking' Brown! Ian was exceedingly keen and because of this, the bosses loved him. He was the only Manchester-speaking Scotsman I had ever known.

I got changed into my damp, smelly new uniform and after squashing banana into my beard to give it the mucus look, I felt ready for the task ahead. Prior to being dropped off into the war zone, Ian Brown and myself were given instructions about what we could and couldn't do. We were handed enough cash to buy a bit of grub and; if the opportunity arose, some Class A drugs. The initial stage, was to become part of the street furniture; this meant walking many miles and being seen by as many criminals as possible.

As I walked into the town centre, I called in a newsagents' shop to buy some chocolate milkshake—the drink of a heroin addict. And while Ian Brown waited outside the shop doing his Happy Mondays impression; the Asian shopkeeper served me and with curiosity in his eyes said;

'You two lads are new around here, aren't you?'

'Fuck me' I thought, 'we haven't even entered the town and someone has already sussed us out as being cops.'

I didn't bother telling Ian what the shopkeeper had said, as I didn't want us both being paranoid as fuck. I convinced myself that the shopkeeper wanted to protect his shop from thieving heroin addicts and his conversation was his way of keeping us on his side. The first week was mainly getting our faces known. I couldn't be arsed we hadn't bought any drugs, as I knew a patient approach would be the best way to approach the task in hand. Addicts and drug dealers in this town were suspicious of new faces and had to trust us before they would have anything to do with us. I could see the enthusiasm of the local officers fading, a lot of planning had gone into this operation and the local officers must have been secretly thinking if we were the right people to put on the streets to buy drugs.

Although the pressure was on, I felt more comfortable with my new identity. Every morning I would run up the hill which Sergeant Harwood had introduced me to. Once I reached the top I did press-ups and made sure I covered my hands and face in mud; which was becoming ingrained into my skin, I then ran down the hill and drove to the meeting place. En-route to the meeting place my mind would race, worrying about the operation, and if I was convincing enough to pass as a heroin addict. 'Paul' would also think about his other identity of being a husband and a father to two young children. This identity would travel home every night to his loving family and would try to explain why he looked so shitty. His children were not too concerned about the new heroin addict in their life, however during the next few months, as his appearance became worse, they told him they didn't want him to drop them off at school or attend any parents' evenings which made the father identity extremely angry with Bastard Paul.

Kath was so supportive and held everything together, just as she did whilst I was investigating the gangs in the tower-block area; it was a good job she was a tough cookie. The second week started pretty much the same as the first week ended, walking around getting our faces known. I knew it was coming together and I looked the part when I walked alongside a row of parked cars waiting at red traffic lights. Most of the occupants of the cars were probably on their way to work, but just on the off chance that one car might contain drug dealers, I glanced into each car. One of the first cars I looked into contained two well-dressed women, the driver of the vehicle mouthed the word 'urghhh!' The occupants in the remaining cars looked at me in disgust as they locked their doors from inside.

Myself and Ian walked on and loitered around a telephone box, because undercover officers buying Class A drugs still used the telephone boxes to place their order, even though the addicts didn't queue up at them anymore. This would change a few years later because nearly all addicts had access to a mobile phone. Saying that, it took the 'junkie world' about ten years to catch up with the Information Age. It was refreshing to use the telephone box and took me back to being a child again; the urine and tobacco smells brought back happy memories. As we lingered outside the phone box, an addict approached myself and Ian. He walked with a limp and used a walking stick to assist him; this lad was the real deal with greyish-yellow coloured skin, which someone who isn't an addict cannot replicate.

With a slimy look towards us, he spoke; 'Are you two scoring?'

He gave me the creeps, but I couldn't afford to let myself judge him like a straight-head would.

'Yea' we both told him, 'but we can't get through.'

The addict, whose name I later found out to be Wayne, offered to phone a dealer for us. We had lined ourselves up for the oldest trick in the book, but we had to take a chance. Wayne put the order in for us with his dealer and we gave him £20 for 3 bags of heroin.

'Just wait here, the dealer will kick off if he doesn't know you,' Wayne said, as he limped off out of our sight.

Like Dumb and Dumber, Ian and I waited and waited and waited...

My suspicion about this slimy sod was correct. Wayne never intended to come back to us and had probably injected our money up his arm before we went back to inform our bosses that we had spent £20 of the police forces' budget, with nothing to show for it.

One thing our £20 did buy though was a story; something to speak to other addicts about. Like most people in society, addicts loved a drama; and our sob story about Wayne ripping us off would prove more useful than if he had bought drugs for us. From the moment Wayne ripped us off, everything became realistic. The day after being conned by Wayne; we approached addicts asking if they had seen him, we then told each one of them our story of being ripped off. Some found it funny that we fell for this trick, but one or two felt sympathetic; and gave us their dealers' telephone numbers.

'Tell them you know us and you will be okay,' they explained.

The first number given to us was for Irish. A group of Asian males used the name 'Irish' for their drug dealing line. Most of these males lived on an estate filled with terraced houses. These houses were built during the industrial revolution when the mills boomed—the mills closed, employment vanished, and the houses became neglected. We called this estate the Tree Estate because each of the terraced streets was named after a different tree.

I went to a phone box just outside this estate and nervously phoned the number given to us by the addicts. Although it was only a phone call; my heart pounded, wondering what the dealer would to say.

The call connected and I popped my twenty pence pieces into the coin slot;

Dealer— 'Yeah?'

Paul— 'It's Paul, can you sort me?'

Dealer— 'Who? I don't know fucking Paul.'

My heart pounded faster; I explain to him a mate had given me his number.

Dealer — 'Listen, I don't know what you're on about, I'm not a fucking dealer so don't phone me again, you fucking cunt.' He then ended the call.

'Fuck me,' I thought, 'I even sound like a copper.'

Maybe I should have used a fake Manchester accent; like Ian who looked at me as though I was the biggest loser walking the planet.

The following day something unexpected happened, which would open the doors to the local drug dealers. I began to feel comfortable walking the streets: the same old woman cleaning her step, the filthy net curtains of her next-door neighbour which only moved when a Rottweiler dog heard us walking past, then attempted to barge through the living room window, a group of Asian males stood outside a corner shop, swapping mobile numbers, trying to look and sound gangster, the public walking about trying to ignore how their community had turned into a shit hole. I was sure that the males were drug dealers, but even these males had stopped staring at us and seemed to accept us walking through their 'ghetto.'

As we walked past the shop, the noise of a high-speed car travelling behind me broke the normality of everything and wakened my senses. A silver Ford Focus car slammed on its brakes on the road at the side of myself and Ian; from experience this would be drug dealers in a hire car, or cops. Two males in their twenties pounced out of the vehicle and walked, almost strutting towards myself and Ian. I immediately identified they were plain clothed cops, who wore body armour over their sweaters with radios and handcuffs attached to their body armour. Another male and a female got out of the car to join their colleagues; they dressed the same and I got the impression the cops intended to take control of us.

'What are you doing around here, lads?' barked one of the male cops. He was trying to come across as friendly but I could see behind his eyes he wanted a result, to prove he was a good cop.

'Erm; just walking,' I answered trying not to sound sarcastic, but I felt the officers thought I was.

All four officers surrounded me, and one of them took the lead.

'Look mate, (cocky pause, followed by a smug look) I know we don't look like cops, but we are,' he said whilst pointing towards his body armour with both index fingers.

As I looked at the four officers who all wore Karrimor clothing, I nearly wet myself laughing inside; they couldn't have looked more like cops if they tried. I knew cops wore this clothing, because it was cheap walking gear, bought from the sports soccer shop. The only exception to the Karrimor outfits, were the jeans worn by a female police officer which had a shiny spangled pattern on the arse pockets. Cops on divisions who wore their own clothes sometimes referred to themselves as being undercover cops. Even I didn't consider myself as a true undercover, and here I was being grilled by a load of cops who thought I was a criminal. After composing myself, one of the officers, who I later found out was the Sergeant and supervisor of this local pro-active unit took over and pointed his finger in my face.

'I know you, I've locked you up for burglary.'

This comment even made Ian grin, something he normally prevented himself from doing. Seeing Ian grin, made me do the same and upon seeing this the Sergeant saw red and looked embarrassed in front of his subordinates; he needed to regain power.

'Take you coat off,' he said. It was freezing cold weather, but I followed his instructions.

'Now take your jumper off.' Again I complied with his instructions and I immediately started to shiver through my thin t-shirt. With all the physical training I didn't have much meat on me, and the cold weather felt like needles sticking into me. The remaining three officers, who looked as though they were uncomfortable about this situation tried to distance themselves from the actions of their Supervisor, by nervously passing my coat around between themselves and searching its pockets. Because there were no pockets in my jumper; they threw this on the pavement.

Unhappy with the fact they had found nothing in my coat, one officer wanted to search the pockets of my three striped tracksuit bottoms;

'Turn around,' he ordered, looking to get the Sergeants approval.

Wanting to get this illegal search over as quickly as possible, I went along with whatever was asked of me. As soon as I turned around, the officer pushed me in my back forcing my face against the red brick wall of the end terraced house next to where we were stopped.

'Put your arms to the side and spread your legs.'

I knew the procedure well and passively went along with the further instructions; I also pitied this lad having to put his hands through my skanky pants. As he was conducting his search, I heard another car pulling up, to my surprise four more male cops jumped out of it; they all wore Karrimor clothing, with body armour over their sweaters. These lads seemed even cockier, probably because they didn't have a Sergeant in their car, to reign them in.

One of the males who had a skinhead interrupted the cop who was searching me.

'I'll take over,' he told his colleague in a Scouse accent.

Confused, I turned around to see what was going on, at which point the skinhead cop slammed me against the wall.

'Stay fucking still!' he instructed through gritted teeth and with his hardest sounding voice. My mind immediately flashed back to being an eleven-year-old child, when the Everton fans glassed the grown man.

All the officers seemed to take their frustration out on me, probably because I was a lot taller than Ian, who stood to one side smirking, I wondered if Bin Laden would be getting this much attention—and I had done nothing wrong.

As we had bought no drugs, the search was negative, so the officers had to dig deep with their universal wisdom to get me for something. The officer with the skinhead changed his approach,

'Are you on drugs?' he quizzed in a sickly patronising tone.

'No officer,' I replied. 'But if you lot can just leave me, I'll try to buy some,' I thought.

Not believing me he demanded to look at my arms,

'Are they track marks?'

I looked at my arms and saw nothing, I explained my findings to the officer who couldn't be convinced.

'Yes, he's got track marks,' he proudly told his fellow officers. At which point, my head rocked; I could only imagine he wanted to believe it, or he was proving to the other officers he possessed knowledge of the drugs world. Track marks are when addicts inject drugs into their veins which causes the veins to collapse, leaving what I can only describe as a pen line along the skin.

I asked the skinhead if I could put my jumper and coat back on as by this point I was freezing to death and my nose ran; the skinhead appeared to be thinking about an answer, but before he could speak the Sergeant shouted,

'No, we've not finished with you yet.' I spent the rest of the operation suffering from flu, thank you very much, Sergeant.

Not finding anything to arrest me for, the Sergeant asked me my name, date of birth and if I had any tattoos, so I supplied him with the details I had created and showed him my 'skins never' tattoo. An officer used his radio to check my details on the police national computer; which came back no trace. Also, the only person having a 'skins never' tattoo was a woman in the South of England—I wasn't the only living dickhead. The details I provided didn't match up with someone who has a criminal record; and not trusting what I had told him, the Sergeant asked me what my star sign was. People who give the police a false date of birth don't normally know the star sign for this false date of birth, luckily, I used a date of birth near to my correct one.

'Aquarius,' I exclaimed; feeling proud of myself, but pissing off the Sergeant even more.

Ian chuckled; 'Who does he think he is, Mystic Meg?'

The officers having used all their wisdom, still couldn't find a reason to arrest me, so no pats on the back for them. Reluctantly, on the command of the Sergeant they got back into their cars; but desperate to have the last word, the Sergeant angrily turned in my direction with the warning;

'Don't worry, we'll meet again.'

'Fuck me, he's Vera Lynn now,' I whispered to Ian with a smirk.

I put my upper clothing back on and when I stopped shivering, I thought.

'I'm sure we will one day.'

Once the cops drove off, we continued on our path, making our way to a nearby phone box to get ourselves spotted, and hoping to bump into some addicts. Whilst walking, I began to hate the police for the way they had treated me, and wondered if I treated people the same way when I was the cop identity. After an hour of loitering, we walked back through the Tree Estate and as we approached the Asian males stood outside the shop, I noticed they were staring at us. I felt like there was a big arrow above my head with the words 'give this fucker a hard time' written on it. Preparing myself for the worst, I walked past the males and just as we passed one of the males spoke.

'Fuck me, boys, the filth gave you a hard time, didn't they?'

The wannabe gangster look was no longer on their faces, as they wanted to make money from the two new customers stood in front of them. After small talk, the main lad out of the group put his hand in his pocket, then passed Ian what looked like a business card. I didn't ask what was on the card, but after we walked out of sight of the males, Ian pulled it out of his pocket and showed me; my face must have lit up when I saw a telephone number on the card and underneath it, the word 'Irish.'

It would have been desperate to phone the number the same day, so the following day we walked just outside the Tree Estate and made a telephone call from a phone box. It seemed so easy; after explaining who we were, we received instructions to wait in a back alley near to the phone box. An Asian male approached us on foot; he did not speak to us until Ian Brown asked for '2b and 2 white'. The male produced 2 small bags of brown powder which was heroin and 2 small wraps of white powder, which was crack cocaine. The money was given to the dealer, and we separated in opposite directions.

A few more days passed, and on each occasion, we purchased Class A drugs from the same dealer; again the observation team hadn't obtained footage of the dealer. Then one day, Ian took leave for a special occasion, so I phoned the Irish line and was instructed to wait in a cobbled back alley between two rows of rundown terraced houses; the dealer said he would meet me there. I limped into the back alley and sat on the floor leaning against the back wall of a terraced back yard and waited. After five minutes an addict joined me in the alleyway.

'Are you waiting for Irish?' he asked,

'Yea,' I couldn't be arsed to get into a full-blown conversation, as I didn't feel the need to.

The addict didn't want to speak, so I played with the broken glass bottles scattered across the floor, trying to dig the tar from in-between the cobbles. More addicts entered the alleyway, known as 'stacking up.' The dealers 'stacked' the addicts up and although many customers attracted attention, it was less risky for the dealers to do this instead of doing ten different deals. The addicts who were stacked in the alleyway got bored waiting and only stayed because they needed their fix. To entertain everybody, one elderly addict gave us a free training lesson on the subject of injecting Class A drugs. He showed everybody the collapsed veins on his arms and legs, then proud as punch he dropped his trousers, bent over and showed the addicts where he now injected his drugs—up his arsehole! Other addicts took their study lesson seriously until the focus changed when an Asian male walked into the other end of the alleyway—this was the start of the addicts' 100 metre dash. Like the Arabian derby, the addicts set off down the alleyway to get their drugs, because I needed to get to my feet, the addicts had a head start. I wasn't bothered as I wanted to meet the dealer without the addicts surrounding me. It was funny to see, because none of the addicts ran, but walked at speed pushing in front of each other with their arms swinging faster than their legs.

At the finishing line, the drug dealer waited with his two minders who only looked about 15-years-old. As the addicts gathered around the dealer, he looked flustered;

'No, give me a bigger one,' demanded the addicts after being handed crack cocaine.

'I was before him—'

'No I was before him.'

After the rush had gone, I was alone with the dealer.

'One and one,' I asked, but just as he was going to serve me, one of his minders grabbed his attention.

'He's a cop,' one of the young lads said whilst pointing at my face. The dealer looked at me waiting for a reaction. It took a couple of seconds to react because my heart had stopped.

'Of course I am you little prick, that's why I'm buying fucking gear,' I jokingly said to the young lad whilst showing him the back of my hand and pretending to hit him.

The dealer began to laugh then handed me my drugs.

Over the next week, several Irish line dealers turned up; a few appeared to be under duress to deal.

After the operation a kind officer told me that one of the dealers, who was pleasant to talk with, hung himself in prison six months after the operation concluded. I felt for this lad as he spoke about his new-born child every time we met. This played on my mind for a few years, but I needed to focus on how I had stopped him dealing dangerous drugs to vulnerable people.

In-between scoring from the Irish line, an addict gave me a name and the drug dealing location of another dealer called Barry—this was his actual name! Barry was a popular name for children born in the sixties, he looked like he had been a punk rocker, done weightlifting and he still sported a crewcut style haircut. Barry didn't look like a drug dealer; maybe a beer drinker, but desperate times lead to desperate acts, I suppose. As we didn't have his number, myself and Ian just hung around near to the location where he dealt drugs, which was the back streets near to where he lived. By this time, I had developed fully blown man-flu following the illegal search which the local officers carried out. I coughed phlegm constantly and was sweating profusely. I couldn't stand upright in the back streets, so I lay down and waited. This was not an act, I was ill and when Barry first walked past us, he pushed his shoulders back and shouted;

'Who the fuck are you?'

'It's Paul, Wayne told us you would sort us out.'

Wayne hadn't said a word, but I thought I'd get one over on the thieving skank.

After playing the hard man and asking us a few shitty questions, he mellowed, served us up and gave us his telephone number. If Barry didn't turn up, it would be his girlfriend, who was also unpleasant towards us. We didn't need to spend much time with Barry because we quickly gathered enough evidence to convict him.

Another user gave us the telephone number for the 'Charlton Line', who operated a few streets away from where Barry served us, and opposite where the Irish line operated. This was always tricky because dealers would get touchy if addicts bought from different dealers. Not only did they lose their 'hard earned' money, if addicts moved from one dealer to another the dealers got suspicious. Even though I was walking around like a drugged-up zombie, I became excellent at seeing other dealers—before they saw me.

The 'Charlton line' drug dealers who drove around in hire cars, asked users to get in their car and drove addicts through the streets for a short distance whilst the deal was being done. The operation team were uncomfortable that I was to get into a vehicle, as it was deemed to be too dangerous. I pointed out to my handler how it would be suspicious if I didn't get in to the Charlton dealers' vehicle, so I would check it out first to see if it was safe first. Surprisingly, this course of action was allowed and the following day I took my dog Charlie to work. 'Charlie' was a little scruffy mongrel who spent months on that operation with me. It made me so angry when he didn't get an award for what he went through; my award went under the bed with the rest, Charlie's wouldn't have.

I phoned the Charlton line who didn't ask questions; they told me to wait in an alleyway behind a row of terraced houses, opposite to the Tree Estate. It was the middle of winter and pissing down with rain; I made my way with Charlie who looked so pissed off because I had taken him out of his nice comfy bed to walk around the shitty streets to help me buy drugs. I waited for what seemed a lifetime in the backings; the longer it went on, the more I risked the Irish dealers walking past and questioning me why I wasn't buying from them anymore. Even though there was enough evidence gathered on Irish, I would still dip in now and again to buy drugs from them to keep them sweet. Forty-five minutes later, I was wondering if the Charlton line even existed; as they still hadn't turned up. I felt guilty because Charlie was staring at me and appeared to be thinking about reporting me to the RSPCA. The public walked past me staring in disgust, thinking how shitty the area they lived in had become. I walked back to the phone box and wasted another pound's worth of twenty-pence pieces. As I entered the phone box; Charlie, now sheltering from the rain, curled up in the corner; lying on the damp, piss stained floor scattered with fag ends, he looked sad. I made the call and I must have sounded so fucked off, more for Charlie than myself.

'Hi, it's Paul, where the fuck are you?'

'Sorry mate, I'll be there soon,' came the reply from a male who sounded as though he had forgot about me.

I realised after a few weeks of buying from the Charlton line this was normal. I don't think I ever received a good service from them and considered putting a complaint in to their superiors. He advised me to wait in the same place, so reluctantly, I did; Charlie almost made me drag him out of the stinky phone box.

Another thirty minutes passed in the back alley when a car came speeding down the backings, knocking wheelie bins to one side. It came to a sudden stop at the side of where I stood, splashing me with filthy water which had been collecting in a pothole. The driver of this car was a male in his twenties who wound the driver's window down, then shouted, ordering me to get in the vehicle. I walked over to his window and shoved my mucus-filled beard to the opening of the window;

'I can't get in, my dog will shit all over your car,' I warned him.

The passenger who was another male in his twenties looked disgusted, either with me or the thought of my dog shitting in his car, he mumbled something to the driver.

'Okay, what do you want?' the driver enquired.

I ordered 2 bags of heroin and two bags of crack; this was spending more money that I needed to, but I had to make the dealers feel I was worth coming out to. The exchange took place through the gap in the driver's window and as soon as the deal took place the driver drove off, shouting;

'Don't bring your fucking dog next time.'

I'm sure I could see Charlie smiling and thinking, 'Thank fuck for that.'

I reported back to my handler how the Charlton dealers were just wannabe gangsters trying to earn a few quid and they posed no threat. It took a few days to allow it, but it was agreed I could get into a vehicle. I put a call into the Charlton line and as usual they were 45 minutes late, the same vehicle and driver pulled up in the backings and I got into the rear seat. The car drove around the corner and the front seat passenger exchanged drugs for my cash. It was as simple as that.

On one occasion we telephoned the Charlton Line and were instructed to wait in the backings as usual, but this time to wait further down the street, because the locals had been telephoning the police about drug users waiting behind their houses. So, we waited in this new location, which was even more open to the public's gaze than it was before. It was extremely cold and rained so much, our clothes were soaking wet through and the odour we produced even made me feel sick. The Charlton dealers didn't turn up for an hour and a half. I began to think to myself how much I was hating this job, even Ian

Brown lacked enthusiasm, which I hadn't seen before. A few members of the public drove past, stopped and stared at us in a vigilante manner. I could understand the residents, because I wouldn't appreciate addicts hanging around where I lived, and leaving needles lying around for children to pick up, I wish I could have told them I was there to help. Charlton finally turned up; the deal was done, and we went our separate ways. The following day; the Sergeant who ran the operation showed us a police printout, created after a member of the public had phoned the police.

DRUG DEALING
There are two 'white rats' with a dog, walking around the streets. I think they are buying drugs from people in a hire car.

To have fooled the public into believing we were genuine heroin addicts was a boost; but I wanted this operation to finish. The public were right in their observations because I began to feel like a stinking rat; skulking around the streets. Several other dealers working for the Charlton line served us drugs, some turned up on foot making it easier to gather video evidence. They were mostly lads in their twenties; dealing to pay for their own weed and cocaine, and to maintain their wannabe gangster lifestyle.

The last dealer we encountered was 'Bluey,' who we stumbled across. We were walking to catch a public bus after scoring drugs off the Charlton dealers, when a shitty old Ford Cortina stopped at the side of us. Inside the vehicle were two Jamaican males who asked if we wanted to buy drugs. They came from out of town and were poaching on other dealer's patches. I told them we had no money, which was true, this didn't defer the Jamaican driver who handed me a small rock of crack cocaine and a small bag of heroin. He said it was a tester and if we thought it was good quality, we could call him on a telephone number which he then provided us with. A part of me was thinking 'great, at least we look the part after months of being on the streets,' another part of me thought, if I was a real addict I would find it so hard to stop when there were wankers like these two offering freebies. We spent the last week of the operation gathering evidence on Bluey which proved to be easy; as they served us drugs near to the house where they lived.

The operation ended and I was exhausted; the flu and mental pressure had taken all my strength. Paul was yet another identity the ego had recruited, who of course, also suffered from PTSD—I wanted to curl up and die.

I travelled home, shaved my hair and shaved my beard, which reminded me of being a 11-year-old skinhead again. My children kissed me on my freshly shaven cheeks, which they didn't do when I was sporting a scruffy beard. My wife cuddled up to me in bed now I didn't look like a rapist anymore. Kath and my children appeared relieved that Paul was no longer in their lives, but I wasn't so lucky—Bastard Paul was ingrained into my mind and didn't want to leave.

DRUGS CASE UPDATE
30 people sentenced to a total of 100 years' imprisonment.

Following this operation, the unit allowed me to take a few unofficial days leave. In these few days I needed to erase the 'Paul' identity before going back to my division. But with no psychological therapy being offered; returning to the 'normal' frame of mind was impossible in such a short period.

Sergeant Harwood had been moved over to the divisional drugs unit to improve their detection rates and when I returned to my police station, he asked me to join him on his unit. As usual, Sergeant Harwood put his heart and soul into the drugs unit and we soon became involved with some high-profile arrests.

Not long after joining the divisional drugs unit, I was approached and asked if I was interested in going onto the streets full time. For the next two years I couldn't go near to a police station and spent several months posing as a heroin addict, working alongside a younger officer. This officer was the most switched-on police officer and the most realistic undercover officer I had met. He was far more natural as an addict than I was and played an important role in crushing a large drugs ring.

Officers gathered evidence on hundreds of low-level drug dealers during this two-year spell, but even if we had arrested these dealers for another two hundred years, not much would have changed. Low level drug dealers were replaced at the drop of a hat and it was the vulnerable members of society forced into this role.

I have recently read a book 'Good Cop, Bad War' written by an ex-undercover cop, Neil Woods and JS Rafaeli. Speaking as a police officer, I would say there are some important points written within this book and the campaign for legal regulation of drugs should be reinforced from high up. I wish Leap UK all the best with their campaign because the illegal drugs trade destroys everything it touches.

I can understand why the war on drugs took place in the eighties and nineties because the public would have criticised the police for not doing anything and society wasn't wise enough to regulate the drugs. But something needed to be done, the new drugs scene became the scourge of society and people were burying their heads in the sand. In situations which frighten the public, it is the police who they look too for answers and this happened during this period. I hope the efforts police officers put in during this time prevented some members of society becoming addicted to Class A drugs. But it is now time to progress before there is any further collateral damage caused by the war on drugs, which has proved unsuccessful in the United Kingdom and with experts like Leap UK, we are now ready for the change.

During my time associated with the war on drugs; I witnessed people shot, kidnapped and assaulted. Vulnerable addicts who have committed suicide after being forced to deal drugs to feed their habit. Police officers sent to jail after becoming corrupted. An undercover police officer become addicted to heroin and sent to jail for stealing property to feed his habit. Police officers and their families torn to pieces. Eight police officers surrounding and searching a member of the public just because he looked like a drug user. All this has happened whilst the most violent members of our society became wealthier. Something needs to change because my concerns about society becoming the 'gangsters' paradise,' have become reality.

Before I left the undercover unit, I worked as an operational officer looking after the welfare of undercover officers who had been deployed in a town near to where I lived. These officers gathered evidence on a person, who they linked to the supply of Class A drugs; I felt sick to the pit of my stomach when I found out the person they were investigating was my childhood friend Chris. I drove home that evening in silence, remembering the fun times I spent with Chris and wondered how we had both turned out so mixed-up.

I couldn't return to the drugs unit because an officer had sold information to the local drug dealers and as a result the supervision dis-banded the drugs unit.

My new role was to be a uniformed neighbourhood officer on my division. I was to cover a large council estate in one of the most deprived areas within the force. I wasn't looking forward to performing this role as I'd been away from uniformed policing for too long and I struggled to adapt to the role of a police officer.

My new police post was in a one-bed flat, two floors above a chip shop, one floor above a heavy cannabis user and in the middle of a run-down council estate. Our flat wasn't an everyday flat; it had been converted, allowing officers to access the police database on two computers. Chairs and desks filled the living room and the flat wouldn't be secure unless to be fitted with a good quality security alarm.

As I entered the council flat on the first morning, I was greeted by a police community support officer called Mason. Sat in the office was my new partner, David, who had served in the police service for 28 years and was on a wind-down. There were also two younger police constables and another PCSO, whose beat adjoined the area which myself, Dave and Mason would be working. My new Sergeant wasn't present, he only had two years' service remaining and kept out of the way as long as his officers didn't bring him any trouble.

Mason was an ex-soldier who had toured Northern Ireland and served in the Falklands war. Although I hadn't worked with many PCSOs, I took to Mason. However, because of his military conditioning, he was focused, but very intense. Mason drove the police officers insane with his polished boots and his regimented ways. David later proved to be excellent at dealing with the public, but he was putting his feet up and only went out of the office if he really needed to. The other two officers mimicked David and all three officers would turn out together in a police car if they really needed to.

As I had been trawling the streets every day in the undercover unit, I found this style of policing difficult to deal with and couldn't sit waiting for jobs to come in. Mason cycled around his beat all day and told the bobbies they were lazy. The officers just told him to 'fuck off.' Mason returned the compliment with a thousand-yard stare, 'No, you fuck off.'

What had happened to the police service I once knew? Why had they withdrawn into the police stations? Why did they not walk the streets anymore? I hadn't seen police walking the streets for years, was the beat bobby extinct?

Then one night whilst watching television, a programme enlightened me.

'Look at those coppers,' Kath said, whilst pointing at the screen. We were watching the television programme 'Life on Mars', a television series about policing in the seventies. During one of the scenes, several uniformed police officers wearing their custodian helmets walked out of the police station.

'That's how it should be, Kath, that's what the public want,' I replied proudly.

'Well why don't you do it, I know its 2010 not 1970, but if it stops you complaining about sitting around, get on the streets and do it.'

Kath set the challenge, why shouldn't I give it a go? I had more experience than when I first walked the beat 20 years previously.

'Right then, I will, Kath,' I told her with excitement in my voice.

'I remember PC Green chasing me when I was a kid, I couldn't tell my dad he had been chasing me, because he would have shouted at me,' Kath said before laughing out loud. Everybody around my age had their own story about the old-fashioned beat bobby, who appeared to know everything happening within the community. The beat bobby was part of the community but when the community spirit disappeared, so did the local police officer.

The following day I worked the afternoon shift and when I entered the office, I saw David sat with the other two police officers chatting about football and Mason cleaning the tyres on his pedal cycle whilst giving the bobbies dirty looks. I logged onto a computer and searched the crime figures on my beat for the previous twelve months. The results were high considering it wasn't a huge area: Burglary 36, robbery 8, criminal damage 176, assaults actual/grievous bodily harm 86, and theft from motor vehicles 15. I kept this information locked away, to compare it with the crimes recorded over the next twelve months.

With the crime figures under lock and key, I needed to prove the good old-fashioned British bobby was what the public needed and it was the most successful method of policing. I put on my black raincoat and my custodian helmet. I checked my boots were polished to a decent standard just in case Mason gave me a uniform inspection, and then I headed for the flat door.

'What the fuck are you doing?' David quizzed, as the younger officers chuckled to each other.

'Doing my job, I can't sit around here all day, David, I'll go insane.'

'Sit down, you crackpot, we will go out in the car later on.'

I had a choice of staying indoors and joining the clique or walking out of the door. Kath had set me a challenge and I knew what I needed to do, so I walked out of the flat. Not being in the clique didn't concern me, but I would need to devise a plan to get the other officers out of the office.

I knew there were no officers walking their beats on my division, but I didn't realize what a rarity the sighting of an officer was on a British street. As soon as I walked down the street, it felt I was in an episode of 'Life on Mars' myself and the public were looking at me through a television screen. Motor vehicles stopped in their tracks as the passengers stared at the strange image walking down the street, drivers sounded the horns of their cars, passengers gave me the thumbs up sign, some even cheered. Had it really been so long since they had seen a police officer on foot patrol?

A few months previously, the public had described me as being a 'white rat' as I skulked around their streets, but now I felt as proud as punch walking the streets in my British police officer uniform. It was a role, an image, because there was no difference in the person dressed as a heroin addict, to the one dressed as a police officer, it was only the public's perception of me which changed.

I continued to walk deep into the estate; the daylight was fading and the air was turning foggy. Mothers grinned as their young children hid behind them looking for protection from the seven-foot figure (including helmet) looming towards them.

'Take him away, officer,' the mothers joked. I always felt the need to reassure the children, so they didn't have nightmares after their mothers told them I would lock them up if they were naughty.

As I walked further down the street, I heard lots of shouting coming from a group of teenagers loitering outside the corner shop, 'Oi, black bastard,' they shouted. I plodded towards the group.

'Did someone shout for help just then?'

'What do you mean, Officer?'

'I'm sure someone shouted.'

'No, it wasn't us, Officer.'

'Well, I'm not interested who shouted, I'm not even interested in who you are, but I'll be walking these streets for the next few years, so....'

'So what, Officer?' one of the youths challenged.

'So, I think we should show respect to each other.'

'What if we don't want to?'

'If you don't, I will find where every one of you live and I will spend every afternoon I can, sat in your living room, watching your television and having a cup of tea with your parents.'

'No, no, no,' they all shouted, 'We won't give you any shit.'

'Think on you don't,' I advised, as I walked away grinning to myself. This was going to be interesting.

I noticed Mason cycling past as I spoke with the teenagers and after I walked away from them he approached;

'Did they give you any shit?'

'No, everything is fine, thanks for backing me up.'

'I'm always here, so give me a shout if you need me,' he added, as he saluted before cycling away.

After walking the streets for several hours, I returned to the flat and saw David and the other officers hadn't moved an inch from where they were seated when I left the office. I needed to work on David to get him out on the streets, so before I went home after finishing my shift I had a few words with him.

'When do you retire, David?'

'A few years, why?'

'You could do with some exercise, so you enjoy your retirement. That beer belly seems to be getting bigger.'

'Cheeky bastard,' David snapped back.

I laughed, as I knew this would do the trick, David had been a keen footballer, but with the heavy drinking he looked anything but sporty.

'Night then,' I shouted, leaving David festering in his chair.

The following day I turned up at the flat for my afternoon shift, but something was different. David looked anxious and as I looked at him, I noticed he had polished his boots.

'Erm, what time you going on your beat?' David asked.

'About ten minutes, I'm just going to check who's been phoning us, why do you ask?'

I had guessed what was coming next, but it gave me pleasure when I heard David almost embarrassingly reply, 'I'll have a walk out with you.'

Mason looked on in shock, 'How the fuck have you done that? He's been sat in that chair for two years?'

'Fuck off, Mason,' David snarled.

Mason checked the brakes on his pedal cycle before leaving the flat, 'See you both out there then,' he smugly shouted as he left.

One police officer walking the beat was hard for the public to comprehend, but having two officers walking the beat, blew their minds.

I had forgotten about bastard Paul and all my other identities. I now concentrated all my efforts on the identity of what some would call an old-fashioned British bobby. Walking the streets with David turned out to be an amazing experience, he was a wise old fox and fantastic at communicating with the public, in particular the elderly. For the last two years he had been sitting on his backside the public missed out on his skills, all because walking the beat wasn't the norm.

If the public informed us of any anti-social behaviour within the community, we would direct Mason to the areas mentioned, and he would circle the group until they moved on, or behaved themselves. Luckily, he wasn't too keen to speak with them because having spent too long in war-zones, he would rather shoot them, than get into an argument. If they gave him any lip, myself and David would take over, which the trouble-makers didn't want.

As time went by, figures proved how recorded crime had reduced and the publics spirits seemed to have lifted. Burglars were aware that we spoke with the community and if we didn't spot the burglars mooching, Mason would spot them then inform us. We didn't need to bang heads against a wall or arrest hundreds of criminals, our presence alone proved to be enough. The reason the residents had telephoned the police about their neighbours and minor offences, was because they had nobody else to talk to. Now that they had two police officers they could rely on, they didn't bother to phone the police as they knew we would sort it the next time they spoke with us.

I had lost interest in investigating drug related offences. I dealt with drug incidents for most of my career and not much had changed. The main complaints from the community about drug activities were, heroin addicts leaving their needles lying around for all to see, groups of people causing anti-social behaviour when they were attending drug dealers' addresses or drug dealers openly dealing on the streets. Apart from these complaints, the community didn't care who injected into their body or who was getting high as a kite.

There were quite a few addicts on our beat, so after being told where the addicts were discarding their hypodermic needles, I waited at this location. A few addicts I knew appeared, looking for somewhere to inject.

'If it's you who have been leaving these needles here, please don't.'

'Sorry, Officer, we won't.'

'It's up to you what you do with your body, but do it in private and don't put people at risk leaving the needles lying around.'

'We won't, sorry, Officer.'

The problem was sorted; they stuck to their word and we received no further complaints from the community about needles. Believe it or not, littering is not a heroin addicts major concern.

Drug dealing was taking place at an end-terraced house and youths who attended the address were causing anti-social behaviour. We walked to this address and two teenagers greeted us; I noticed they wore baseball caps which had a cannabis motif on the front of them.

'Hello, do you live here?' David asked.

'No.'

'What's with the pattern on the caps?'

'Cannabis, innit, and you can do fuck all about it.'

'Well, to be honest, I prefer it if you are stoned, it makes you less aggressive,' I said.

'You're just saying that.'

'I'm not, please don't hang around this house annoying the neighbours.'

The males left the area, looking confused as to why the police officers hadn't challenged their mischief or had stopped and searched them. I had smoked cigarettes and sniffed glue at eleven years of age to blank out the primary wounds and understood why they were smoking cannabis.

I knocked on the door of the end-terraced house but the occupier didn't answer, so we spent the next two hours talking to other residents on the street. If the occupant had peeped through his curtains, he would now know anybody in the street could inform us about his activities. A few days later myself and David re-attended the address; there had been no further calls about anti-social behaviour and after ten minutes speaking to residents in the street, a teenage male came out of the end terrace.

'I believe you was knocking at my door.'

'Yes, we have been, I have heard something has been going on at your address and it is upsetting the people who live in the street.'

'I've not done anything, I swear, Officer.'

'Okay, I'll take your word for it, but please don't annoy the neighbours as you will make me look stupid if things continue. If I find out you haven't changed your ways, I might have to knock harder next time.'

'Okay, Officer, thank you, I get your point.'

There weren't any more calls to the police regarding the end terrace and after the visit, residents in the street informed us the occupant had moved out of the area. A quick call to the landlord made sure he didn't rent the address out to another dickhead. Some supervisors would be fuming with our approach as they craved action. They wanted warrants being executed and people being arrested, to prove to their superiors they were pro-active. If we banged doors in and dragged people out of their houses, the residents would never have experienced peace.

We had been walking the streets for twelve months, so I researched the crime figures and was more than happy with the results: Burglary 20, robbery 4, criminal damage 96, assaults actual/grievous bodily harm 60, and theft from motor vehicles 9. The recorded crimes had reduced, but I could still see room for improvement and wanted there to be no crimes. We continued on for the next twelve months with the same simplistic ways. Gangsters were approaching us, thanking us and informing us their parents felt so much safer having us patrolling the streets. I didn't know how to take these compliments.

I joined a Thai boxing class on my beat and sparred with a few local hard-nuts. I was inspired by a recovering drug addict who ran the group; he was a hard as nails and a fantastic human being. I also learned how to protect myself from the hard-nuts who wanted to knock my block off. Having proven that I could take a few punches, I could persuade these lads about my idea of having the streets crime free. If they were committing crimes, it was elsewhere, as I'm sure they wouldn't want to let myself or David down.

The second year's results proved to be staggering: burglary 2, robbery 0, criminal damage 40, assaults actual/grievous bodily harm 42, and theft from motor vehicles 2.

The figures fell because of a supportive Sergeant who trusted us to do our job. He later received a well-deserved award from the council, for leading the best community team. The modern-day officers may never experience what we did because they are under-staffed and find themselves overburdened with enquiries from the public, who feel the need to phone the police every time somebody gives them a dirty look. It's ironic, but the only traditional police officer the public could see soon, will be the one stood outside Number 10 Downing Street.

The reduction in police service funding resulted in the fall of the police numbers. After two years walking the beat, myself, David and Mason were informed by our Inspector that due to the cuts, we would be moved to separate stations to make the numbers up. He also said we had been selected because there wasn't much crime being committed on our beat. I almost told him all the reasons for this but bit my tongue, his decision was made. David was retiring soon and finished his service on a high, feeling proud of his last few years as a 'real' police officer and was now minus his beer belly. Mason fell out with his new colleagues who didn't 'get' his military ways and the force moved me indoors to investigate the theft of fish, you know the rest.

I realise I've babbled on about how traditional policing works, but I need to get my point across. Traditional foot patrol does work and I would love to see officers walking past my house. This is and always has been the British way.

The vast majority of the British police are the best in the world and with more financial input, which could come from the regulation of drugs, then it wouldn't be too late to reverse policing methods to the traditional ways. This is what the public desire. We shouldn't follow other countries and how they police their communities. If this happens we may as well put the army on the streets. I hope this never happens.

Chapter eight

The recovery

The bag of fish enquiry was a blessing in disguise as it forced me to appreciate life. This is why I titled the book 'A Beautiful Bag of Fish.'

The ego created identities and their thoughts/fish in the 11-year-old football fan, the skinhead, etc. Then came along the drugs cop and the drug addicts, larger and more dominant fish who seemed to be the ones responsible for causing my mental health problems.

These identities created a false-self and a virtual inner world became its home. The glassing incident I saw as the 11-year-old child was the primary wound which solidified the false-self. The true-self, which is pure, radiant, infinite and one with everything, was cast aside.

This is difficult to accept by someone who has a bag crammed full of fish, ranging from great white sharks to slippery eels, who believes in their false-self, but at the same time is desperate to be free from their mental anxiety. This normally results with the person creating another identity/another fish which will try and work out what their own mental health problem is, resulting in the bag of fish becoming even more crammed. However, never try to tell them their thoughts are non-existent or else you might come face to face with their great white shark. In my case consciousness took over by closing my mind. The false-self didn't have a clue what had happened, creating panic as it was in fear of losing its hard work, creating identities and the virtual inner world.

The universal belief is that we are all individual beings. Most beings create a few tiny fish in their virtual inner world. This is fine as it is the play of existence, but there are more and more people in society with bags crammed full of fish, especially everybody involved with the war on drugs. This war affects drug addicts and their families as well as police officers and their families, putting the mental health service under strain.

The false-self deep down knows it is not real; it knows it was created by the mind; it knows it is just an elaborate thought-form, so it feels unsteady and unsafe. Any confusing, traumatic or distressing experience shakes the ego to its core. It constantly fears for its 'life' so it has to develop coping mechanisms, survival strategies and defensive behaviours to strengthen itself and reinforce its position. A lot of physical, emotional and mental energy are utilised in maintaining the ego's belief structures, coping structures and defensive structures.

As the false-self creates new ego structures, it expands into them, identifies with them and becomes one with them. The false-self expands into the structures to create the ego. We then spend the rest of our lives defending our false-self and reinforcing our ego. These behaviours are the cause of all our unnecessary suffering. Many behavioural patterns are essential to life, allowing us to breathe, move, eat, digest, walk, talk, read and drive without giving these tasks our full conscious attention. These patterns start developing as soon as we are capable of learning. But they are not ego structures if we don't identify with them, take them personally or believe they are us.

When I first attended the occupational health unit after the bag of fish enquiry, I needed confirmation I was a loved human being; the conversation went like this:

Occupational health reception: 'Hello, have you got an appointment?'

Self: 'Erm, I'm here to see the welfare unit as I have been having a few problems.'

Occupational health reception: 'Number?'

Self; 'Pardon?'

Occupational health reception: 'Number, I need your collar number to input into the computer.'

The receptionist didn't take her eyes away from the computer screen.

Self: 'Do you not need my name?'

Occupational health reception: 'No, your number is all we need.'

Although the receptionist was fully engrossed in her own virtual inner world and showed no compassion to a human being who was seeking to understand the true-self, the therapist I visited at the occupational health unit showed understanding, compassion and care. He was transparent and clarified his aim, which was to make sure I returned to work and my wellbeing wasn't important to the police service. I understood his predicament because the police paid him to get me strong enough to return to work as a police officer. He wouldn't had lasted long if he pointed me away from the identity of a police officer and towards an awareness of the true-self.

Along with complex PTSD, the force psychiatrist diagnosed me with major depressive disorder and to top it off, my doctor discovered permanent atrial fibrillation, a heart condition brought on by stress. After spending 25 years in the police service; I handed in my police warrant card and with it; I handed in all the identities and the disorders which I had collected whilst working for the police. My heart returned to a normal rhythm through cardio version and the cardiologist told me there was nothing structurally wrong with my heart and it must have been the stress created by the mind which had affected the heart's rhythm. The 'recovery' was complete, although in reality there was never anything wrong with the true-self and nothing to recover from; the issues lived within the false-self.

During the introduction in this book, I enquired if being consciousness was enough. Or was the conditioned mind too addictive? There is nothing more than consciousness. The conditioned mind is a limited version of consciousness, which if overloaded, can cause physical and mental damage to the human being. The conditioned mind although illusory will always appear to be present, but this is the false self and even when the being believes there are no identities/fish remaining, there will always be a camouflaged stonefish waiting to pounce.

Finally — A huge thanks to the special ones in my life.

Crusty — Don't forget to use your brain — Don't condition those children and make sure you come first. x

Mint drop — You had to join didn't you? Make the most of it and learn from my mistakes, I know you will go far. x

Kath — My beautiful, loving, loyal wife — Only you could put up with so much. We have been on a long rollercoaster ride, but we can now jump on the log flume. Smiling for the camera when it ends. x

Everything written in this book is now his-story, it's time to delete the story, switch off and be like the three-year-old Buddha who didn't realise or care what he was, which is....... THAT.

Que sera, sera.

James

33663028R00116

Printed in Great Britain
by Amazon